SIR GAWAIN AND THE GREEN KNIGHT

Sir Gawain and the Green Knight

Translation by Gwyn Jones
Introduction by Priscilla Martin

WORDSWORTH CLASSICS
OF WORLD LITERATURE

This edition published 1997 by Wordsworth Editions Limited
Cumberland House, Crib Street, Ware, Hertfordshire SG12 9ET

ISBN 1 85326 789 9

Typeset in Great Britain by Antony Gray
Printed and bound in Denmark by Nørhaven

INTRODUCTION

We might easily have lost one of the greatest poems in English literature. The anonymous fourteenth-century romance *Sir Gawain and the Green Knight* survives in only one manuscript, which is now in the British Museum. This manuscript contains three other poems, *Cleanness* (or *Purity*), *Patience* and *Pearl* which are probably by the same author, known as the *Gawain*-poet or the *Pearl*-poet. The four have various features in common. They are written in the same Northwest Midlands dialect and in alliterative verse. They seem to show even more stylistic and lexical similarities than are usual in this native and formulaic tradition. They share a linguistic virtuosity unusual at any time or place. Though they exemplify different genres, they manifest the same interests and ideals. *Patience* and *Cleanness* are overtly didactic, expounding these virtues largely by Biblical illustrations of impatience, impurity, and their punishment: the story of Jonah, the parable of the wedding feast, the Flood, the destruction of Sodom and Gomorrah, Belshazzar's Feast and the fall of Babylon. *Pearl* relates a religious vision: a 'jeweller' who has lost a 'pearl' (presumably his infant daughter) in the long grass of the garden (or graveyard) falls asleep and meets her, now a blessed soul in Heaven, who has little sympathy for his grief and instructs him in the true Christian response to bereavement.

Sir Gawain and the Green Knight, though pervaded by the same religious idealism, is a chivalric romance about one of the major heroes of King Arthur's court. Sir Gawain represents Arthur, his court and its values, chivalry, courtesy and Christian civilisation. The story of Arthur, perhaps originating from a sixth-century Romano-British chieftain who briefly halted the Saxon advance to the West, had been developing throughout the Middle Ages. By the fourteenth century it was the 'Matter of Britain', magnificent though ultimately tragic, with its brilliant court at Camelot, its chivalrous brotherhood of knights, its zeal for glory, its valiant quests and romantic love affairs and its Christian values. It joined and succeeded the Trojan War as the seminal European epic. European nations claimed, indeed, to be descended from Troy, to have been founded, like Rome by Aeneas, by exiled Trojan survivors. *Sir Gawain* opens by placing England, Arthur and his knights in this historical perspective: Britain was founded by the eponymous Trojan Felix Brutus, its story has alternated between joy and trouble ('blysse and blunder'), it has bred many heroes and its noblest king was Arthur.

The opening also places the poem in a literary perspective. At the end of the second stanza the poet addresses the audience, suggesting – or using the convention of – oral performance. If they will 'lysten this laye', he will 'telle hit . . . with tonge' as he 'in toun herde'. In an oral culture poets claim to be conserving the traditional rather than creating the original. Although literacy was increasing at the end of the fourteenth century, public recitation was a necessity for the many who could not read and an amenity for the few who could. An illustration in a manuscript of Chaucer's *Troilus and Criseyde* shows the poet reading his work to Richard II and his court. *Sir Gawain* might have been performed at a manor house or castle, even perhaps before the king on one of his visits to the region. The poet uses the native alliterative metre which had survived (or been revived) in the North and West and which was less fashionable in London. But he experiments with it, using in *Pearl* a rhymed stanza and an intricate system of repeated concatenating key-words, and in *Gawain* ending a flexible alliterative stanza of varying length with a 'bob and a wheel', five short rhyming lines. And more than most alliterative poets of the time, he is a courtly writer. He is inspired by the splendour and ceremonial of court life, by its etiquette and hospitality, by feasts, games, dancing and singing, by hunting and competition, by the latest fashions and architecture. Nor is his ideal of courtliness only aesthetic. It is ethical, even theological. *Courtoisie* goes beyond style and manners: it should include piety, compassion, generosity, chastity and courage. For the *Gawain*-poet, as for other medieval writers, God is the source of courtesy and Christ's incarnation its supreme example. In *Pearl* Heaven is revealed as God's court and Mary the queen of courtesy.

The story opens at a time and place of courtly Christian festivity: 'This kyng lay at Camylot vpon Krystmasse'. It is a season of 'blysse'. The court seems a model of all it should be. The word 'all' is repeated several times, and the people are described in superlatives: the knights are the most famous, the ladies the loveliest, the king the highest. The virtues of Camelot are cheerfully explicit and un-examined. The tone is carefree. The people are young and so is the New Year, when it arrives. After mass and gifts there is a great feast, but Arthur's custom on this day is not to eat until he has been served some 'aventurus thyng', some 'mervayle'. As if on cue the Green Knight rides into the hall, bringing with him more than Arthur bargained for, and emanating ambiguity. He – and his horse – are elegantly apparelled. He is slim and well-proportioned but immensely tall. He seems to be 'half' a giant. And, amazingly, he is absolutely green. Does he come in peace or war? He is not in armour but carries in one hand a bough of holly and in the other a huge green and gold axe. The axe seems both menacing and decorative. The holly betokens the peace of Christmas time but, perhaps like the greenness of its bearer, suggests the vast natural world of forests and danger outside the culture and safety of the hall. The Green Knight's words are equally ambiguous. He claims to come in peace but speaks with a contemptuous *bonhomie*. All he wants is a Christmas game. But what does he mean by a game? He proposes that any man brave enough should take his axe, strike him with it and accept a return blow from him a year later. There is a dreadful silence. The Green Knight exults ('is this Arthures hous?'), and the king accepts the challenge himself.

At this Gawain, who has so far in the poem been only a name, asks to replace Arthur as the knight's adversary. The narrative obliquity with which he enters the action is matched by obliquity of style. A test of courtesy complicates the test of courage. Gawain has to put himself forward without seeming to do so. He achieves this in a speech of syntactic complexity unusual in Middle English, especially in the generally loose and paratactic medium of alliterative verse. He presents the challenge as a problem in courtesy: he begins by requesting to leave the table without 'vylanye', deprecates in passing the company's acceptance of the king's acceptance as 'not semly', and ends by appealing to the court to decide if he speaks 'comlyly'. He even manages to offer himself modestly as champion: as the 'wakkest' and 'feblest' in this superlative court, he is the most dispensable; he is empowered only by his relationship to Arthur as the king's nephew; he should by right (as if to pre-empt a stampede) have this position since he asked first. The request is granted and the Green Knight spells out the terms of the contract, both precise and mysterious. Gawain gives his name and promises to meet the knight in a year's time. He points out that he does not know the name of the knight or his court or where he lives. The knight says he will answer – or not – after he has received Gawain's blow, and does indeed give an answer of sorts. He holds up his severed head and it tells Gawain to meet him at the Green Chapel and to seek the 'Knight of the Green Chapel'. With that he rides out of the hall, no one knows where.

King Arthur absorbs the shock and keeps up appearances. Since they have had some suitable Christmas entertainment, he can dine. 'Now sir, heng vp thyn ax', he says to Gawain, domesticating the monstrous in a proverbial phrase which makes it seem commonplace, even comic. The axe is placed over the dais 'bi trwe tytel therof to telle the wonder' and dinner is served. The courtly façade is restored and its forms are observed. But the axe hangs there like a trophy or a sword of Damocles. A sign, but of what? The court returns to merrymaking. But Gawain is under a death sentence if he keeps his word to the Green Knight. He merges back into the court but the last lines of the first section separate him from it: the narrator addresses him directly and underlines both the danger and the duty of 'this adventure'.

The second part of the poem opens with a vivid account of the procession of the seasons, their pace seeming to accelerate as the year runs away and carries Gawain ever closer to his grim meeting.

> A yere yernes ful yerne and yeldes neuer lyke,
> The forme to the fynisment foldes ful selden.

> A year passes full quickly and never yields its like.
> Seldom the beginning accords with the end.

The annual cycle is predictable but the end of the year is not. The poem has both a linear and a circular structure: we are aware of the recurring rhythm of the seasons and the evanescent beauty of this crucial year which may be Gawain's last. It is charted not only by the natural but also the liturgical calendar. The feast of Christmas is followed by the fast of Lent. At Michaelmas Gawain thinks of his journey but waits till All Souls' Day, the festival of the dead.

The next morning Gawain is armed and sets forth. The arming is one of the most elaborate descriptions in a richly descriptive poem. It is also one of the most overtly symbolic passages in a richly symbolic poem. The arming of the hero is a traditional motif in heroic poetry, found first in the *Iliad*. It is appropriated and transformed by St Paul in a passage of detailed Christian symbolism (*Ephesians* 6: 11–17): the Christian is to put on 'the whole armour of God', and particular moral significance is attributed to each piece of it. Gawain's armour is magnificent, costly and fashionable. But the poet spends most time (and points out that he is willing to delay the narrative in the interests of explication) on the meaning of a sign on Gawain's shield, the five-pointed star called the 'pentangle' or star of Solomon. Solomon, according to this poem, used it to betoken truth 'bi tytle' (the term Arthur applied to the meaning of the axe). The English, because it can be drawn continuously, call it the 'endeles knot'. In its geometric stability and perfection it implicitly contrasts with the flux and contingency of human life, in which the end is rarely like the beginning. Five is a circular number, producing a figure ending in itself whenever it is squared. It is a sacred number and (for obvious reasons) basic to our system of arithmetic. The fiveness of the pentangle suits Gawain, who is faithful in five ways five times over: faultless in his five senses, never failing in his five fingers, placing all his faith in the five wounds of Christ, taking all his courage from the five joys of Mary and pre-eminent in the five virtues of 'fraunchyse', fellowship, cleanness (or chastity), courtesy and pity. Armed thus in chivalric splendour and Christian principle Gawain departs on his quest.

His journey to the Northwest (the poem's own area) is fraught with every kind of trial. He asks again and again about the Green Knight of the Green Chapel, but nobody has ever seen a green knight. He contends with wild animals and the perils of fairy tales: wolves, bulls, bears, boars, dragons, wodwos (forest monsters) and giants. Yet his victories over these traditional hazards are listed briefly, almost comically, as if the hero of romance can be relied upon to take them in his stride. The poet dwells rather on the emotional privation and the realistic problems of the winter journey: the loneliness and the cold. But as Christmas approaches these miseries are dwarfed by another anxiety. Gawain is afraid that he will miss mass at such a holy season and on Christmas Eve he prays to the Virgin Mary to guide him to some lodging. As soon as he makes the sign of the cross, as if by magic a magnificent castle appears. It seems almost too perfect.

Gawain is received with the utmost warmth and

courtesy. Everyone, from the porter at the gate to the lord of the castle, is delighted to welcome him. They know of his reputation and are thrilled to entertain the great Gawain. But his reputation – which they might have picked up from other Arthurian romances – is somewhat at odds with the knight who wears the pentangle. They think of Gawain as a lover and expect a demonstration of flirtatious courtly gallantry from him.

Gawain can play this game when required. But his devotion is to the Virgin and 'clannes' is among the five virtues symbolized by the pentangle. In revising the traditional character of this hero the poet offers an implicit critique of traditional Arthurian romance and the ethic of chivalry, the convention that the good knight should be a good lover. This romance presents the Christian knight as an exemplar of chastity, though it will demonstrate that his virtues involve more tension and conflict than the continuous diagram of the 'endeles knot' might suggest.

The potential conflict between courtesy and chastity is realised at the castle. The Green Knight proposed his bargain as a trial of Arthur's court, a test of Gawain's courage and truth to his word. So when the lord of the castle urges him to stay until the holiday ends at New Year, he explains that he must leave to try to find the Green Knight of the Green Chapel. His host replies that the Green Chapel is less than two miles away. On New Year's Day a guide will escort him towards it. Meanwhile Gawain is to relax in the castle and sleep late while he himself goes hunting each day. He too proposes a bargain: that each evening they should exchange what they have won.

There are obvious parallels and contrasts between the two bargains. They are based on traditional plots known as the Beheading Game and the Exchange of Winnings.

But they suggest different kinds of narrative. The first is heroic, grotesque, supernatural; the second courtly, convivial and more like a 'game'. In combining them the poet invests the heroic with an air of comedy and hints that the cheerful social milieu of the court is morally as testing and perilous. Ordinary domestic life has its trials, ordeals and ethical choices, perhaps the more demanding because more private and insidious.

This is dramatized in three scenes in Gawain's bedroom, which are framed by three scenes of hunting. While the lord pursues deer, boar and fox on three successive days, his wife pursues their guest. Like the Green Knight, she questions the reputation of Arthur's court when its most gallant representative fails to respond to her advances. The recumbent hero does, indeed, look comically undignified as he delicately negotiates his way between the hazards of compromising his chastity, abusing the hospitality of his host or offending his hostess. For three days he succeeds in giving the lady no more than kisses, which he duly exchanges each evening for the quarry her husband has won. But on the third day Gawain keeps something back. He has accepted a green girdle which the lady says has magical power to save his life, and he rides off to keep his appointment on New Year's Day armed with green girdle as well as pentangle.

In the climactic denouement at the Green Chapel it transpires that the test of chastity in the castle was crucial. If Gawain had failed it, he would have lost his life. He was at fault in accepting the girdle but his motive was the understandable desire for self-preservation. The Green Knight turns out to be unexpectedly generous. His view is that Gawain has acquitted himself very well and should keep the green girdle as a souvenir, a 'token', of his adventure at the Green Chapel. But after an ill-natured or perhaps facetious moment of blaming it all on women (the other side of courtesy and chivalry!), Gawain judges himself harshly and accepts the girdle as a sign of his sin. The Green Knight rides off 'whiderwarde-so-ever he wolde' and Gawain to the court, where he tells his story and explains the girdle as a 'token of untrawthe'. The court, however, laughingly adopts it and all wear it as a mark of the renown of the Round Table. Unlike the 'endeles knot' of the pentangle, it can be tied and untied, variously arranged for various functions. It can fasten or undo a lady's garments, serve as baldric for a man's sword, be badge of shame or honour. Like the Green Knight, the green girdle can be interpreted in different ways.

Gawain has to interpret his experience, and the reader is invited to interpret the poem. From the moment the mysterious and ambiguous Green Knight rides into the court, it continually raises questions of signification. Both pentangle and girdle are described as 'signs', but whereas the poet explicates in detail the symbolism of the fixed geometric form of the pentangle and its application to Gawain, the girdle remains pliable and adaptable to the varying significance placed upon it by the characters. An obvious reading of the adventure – and Gawain's own – would see it as a failure: Gawain leaves the court as the knight of the pentangle, sins and compromises and returns as the knight of the green girdle, bound in perpetuity to his shame. But the Green Knight and the court judge it a success. Both readings could be valid if one should be critical of oneself and generous to others. And perhaps, in a poem full of surprises and re-evaluations, we need not privilege the pentangle in all respects over the green girdle. We are tempted to, because we know where we are with the pentangle: the narrator spells it out for us. Absolute moral guidelines are necessary and reassuring. But life is full of complex problems and confusing choices, like the mazy forests and treacherous castles of medieval romance. A geometrical diagram may be perfect but a human being cannot be. It would be a proud illusion if Gawain thought himself always like the pentangle; perhaps it is a kind of inverted proud humility to claim the girdle as the sign of unending sin. The pentangle is 'endless' but the girdle is not.

The poem ends almost as it began. The last line, before the wheel and concluding prayer, is almost the same as the first. The poem is almost circular, as if it aspires to a perfect form like the pentangle. It is an impressive structure. It opens with the fall of Troy, the founding of Britain, Arthur's court, Christmas, the arrival of the Green Knight, the bargain, the arming of Gawain with the pentangle, his departure and journey. The second castle, with its hospitality and courtesy, its commanding lord, its lovely lady, its celebration of the second Christmas, its games and bargains, its enclosure of metaphorical hunting scenes with literal, both mirrors Camelot and performs circles within circles. The poem ends with the second New Year, the second confrontation of Gawain and Green Knight, the second acceptance of the girdle, the exit of the Green Knight, the journey, the return to Camelot, Arthur's court, the founding of Britain, the fall of Troy. But as we were told much earlier, 'the forme to the fynisment foldes ful selde'. (Seldom the beginning accords with the end.) The poem does not quite end on its first line. Its main action, framed by the two meetings with the Green Knight, occupies not exactly a year but a year and a day. It consists of a hundred and one stanzas as if to suggest that human life is full of new beginnings rather than a closed and perfect form. (*Pearl* also has one hundred and one stanzas, returns a changed protagonist to the opening scene and *almost* ends with its first line.) In its symmetry and asymmetry, its idealism and humour, its reverence for tradition and its critical experiment, its over-arching patterns and vividly sensuous detail, *Sir Gawain and the Green Knight* is one of the most powerful and enjoyable works of late Gothic culture.

Priscilla Martin
St Edmund Hall, Oxford

EDITIONS

Malcom Andrew and R. A. Waldron, *The Poems of the Pearl Manuscript*, London 1978

A. C. Cawley and J. J. Anderson, *Pearl, Cleanness, Patience and Sir Gawain and the Green Knight*, London 1976

J. R. R. Tolkien and E. V. Gordon, *Sir Gawain and the Green Knight*, 2nd edition, revised by N. Davis, Oxford 1967

CRITICAL STUDIES

D. S. Brewer and J. Gibson (eds), *A Companion to the Gawain-Poet*, Cambridge 1977

J. A. Burrow, *A Reading of Sir Gawain and the Green Knight*, London 1965

W. A. Davenport, *The Art of the Gawain-Poet*, London 1978

A. C. Spearing, *The Gawain-Poet: A Critical Study*, Cambridge 1970

E. Wilson, *The Gawain-Poet*, Leiden 1976

MODERN VERSIONS

There have been two film versions by Stephen Weeks, *Sir Gawain and the Green Knight* (1973) and *Sword of the Valiant* (1983). Thames Television presented an adaptation by David Rudkin, directed by John Michael Phillips, *Sir Gawain and the Green Knight*, on 3 January 1991.

Harrison Birtwistle's opera based on *Gawain*, with a libretto by David Harsent, was first performed at the Royal Opera House, Covent Garden in 1991, and revised in 1994. The CD Version (Collins CD 70412) is based on the 1994 production.

Iris Murdoch's novel *The Green Knight* (London, 1993), is a creative modern re-working of the poem and makes explicit reference to it.

Sir Gawain and the Green Knight

1

AFTER THE SIEGE AND THE ASSAULT were ended at Troy, the city broken and burned to brands and ashes, the man who had wrought there devices of treason was tried for his treachery, the veriest on earth. It was the glorious Aeneas and his exalted kindred that afterwards overran kingdoms and became lords of well nigh all the wealth in the Isles of the West. From the time that the noble Romulus betakes him swiftly to Rome, with great pomp he first builds that city and names it with his own name, which even now it retains; Ticius proceeds to Tuscany and sets up his dwellings; Langaberde erects homesteads in Lombardy; and far over the French flood Felix Brutus on many a broad shore establishes Britain with joy.

> Where war and wrack and wonder
> Have made abode betimes;
> And oft since, joy and turmoil
> Have rung their changing chimes.

And when this Britain had been founded by this worthy man, bold ones bred therein, who loved strife and wrought mischief in many a time past. Since that same time more marvels have befallen in this country, and often, than in any other I know of. But of all the kings of Britain that have dwelt here, Arthur was ever the most courteous, as I have heard tell. Therefore I propose to narrate an adventure that befell here, which many men reckon a marvel to observe, and an exploit outstanding among Arthur's wonders. If you will listen but a short while to this lay, I shall tell it forthwith, even as I heard it told among men.

> As is set forth and written
> In story brave and strong;
> Linked with unfailing letters,
> As our custom hath been long.

This king lay at Camelot over Christmas with many a splendid lord, the most excellent of men, all those fine brothers-in-arms of the Round Table, nobly, with rich revel as was fitting and with careless mirth. Full many a time men tourneyed there; these gentle knights jousted full gaily and afterwards repaired to the court to dance caroles. For the feast was the same there the whole fifteen days, with all the meat and the mirth men could devise. Such merriment and glee glorious to hear, joyous uproar by day and dancing at night, all was joy to the top of their bent in hall and chamber for lords and ladies, even as seemed most desirable to them. With all the joy in the world they abode there together, the most famous knights under Christ's own self, and the loveliest ladies that ever lived, and he who maintains the court the comeliest king; for all these fair folk in hall were in the prime of their days.

> The most blessed under heaven,
> The king most lofty of will;
> It were now great trial to mention
> A host so hardy on hill.

While New Year was so young it had come in but the night before, that day the company was served twofold on the dais. From the time that the king came into the hall with his knights, the singing of Mass in the chapel drew to a close. A loud outcry was raised there by clerks and others, Noel celebrated anew, named full often; and afterward the nobles ran out to distribute presents, called out their New Year gifts, gave them by hand, and debated earnestly about those gifts. Ladies laughed aloud, though they had lost; and he that won was not wroth, well you may believe it. All this mirth they made until mealtime. When they had washed them fairly, they went to be seated, the best man ever at the top of the table, as seemed most proper. Queen Guenevere, full gay, was set in the midst, in her place on that precious dais, adorned all about, with fine sendal upon her, and over her head a canopy of choice silk of Toulouse, hangings a-plenty of Tharsian stuff, which were embroidered and set with the finest jewels which might be judged worthy of purchase that day or this.

> The comeliest one to look on
> Glanced there with eyes of grey;
> That ever he saw a lovelier,
> No man with truth might say.

But Arthur would not eat till every one was served. He was so high-spirited for youth and somewhat boyish. His life he liked cheerful, he loved that much the less either to lie or to sit for long, so did his young blood and wild brain stir him. Besides, another custom moved him too, which he had taken on him of his magnanimity: he would never eat on such a festal day ere there was told him a wondrous tale of some adventurous thing, some main marvel he might believe in of princes, arms, or other exploits, or some one besought of him a true knight to join with him in jousting and set him in jeopardy, lay life against life, and each one permit the other, even as fortune would further him, to have the upper hand. This was the king's custom wherever he held court, at each goodly feast among his brave household in hall.

> Therefore with face so hardy
> Valiant and firm he stands;
> So early in that New Year
> Much mirth the king commands.

Thus the brave king himself stands there upright, talking before the high table of courteous trifles. There the good Gawain was placed beside Guenevere, and on the other side sits Agravain à la Dure Main, both sister's sons to the king and true knights. Bishop Bawdewyn begins the table above, and Ywain son of Urien eats along with him. These were found places on the dais and honourably served, and thereafter many a true knight at the lower tables. The first course then came in with a blast of trumpets, with many banners full bright hanging therefrom; a fresh noise of kettledrums with gallant piping, wild and loud trillings awakened noise, so that many a heart was high uplifted at their touches. Therewith came in dainties of most precious foods, fresh meat in abundance, and in so many dishes that it was hard to find room to set before folk on the cloth the silver ware which held the various broths.

> Each man there at pleasure
> Took helpings, nothing loth;
> Twelve dishes to each couple,
> Good beer and bright wine both.

I will tell you no more of their service for the present, for every one may be certain there was no lack there. A second and new noise quickly came near, that a man might have leave to take food. For hardly had the noise ceased but a while, and the first course been duly served in the court, when there hales in at the hall door a dreadful master, of stature's height the biggest in the world; from neck to waist so square and thick, and his loins and limbs so long and big, I fancy he was half a giant on earth, and in any case I reckon him to be the biggest of mankind, and the shapeliest of his size that ever rode horse. For though his body was formidable of back and breast, both his belly and his waist were becomingly small, and all his parts clean conforming, after the fashion he had.

> For men had wonder of the hue
> In his appearance seen;
> He bore himself so fiercely,
> All over vivid green.

And this man and his garments were all arrayed in green: a long close-fitting tunic which stuck to his sides, and above it a merry mantle adorned within with fur trimmed clear to view, the stuff full clean and bright with fair blaunner, and his hood too, which was caught back from his locks and laid on his shoulders. Neat, tight-drawn hose of that same green which clung to his calf, and thereunder handsome spurs of bright gold upon silk embroidery most richly barred, and cross-pieces under the instep where the man rides; and all his raiment truly was bright verdure, both the bosses of his belt and other gay stones which were plenteously set in his brave array, about himself and his saddle, on silk embroidery, so that it were too hard to tell of half the little ornaments which were embroidered thereon, with birds and insects and gay green gaudery, and always gold in the midst. The pendants of his breast-harness, the proud crupper, his molaynes and all the metal that ensued were enamelled; the stirrups he stood in were coloured the same, and his saddlebows behind and his splendid tailstraps, ever gleaming and glancing throughout with green stones. The horse that he rides assuredly a fine one of that same colour.

> A green horse big and heavy,
> A steed full hard to hold,
> Quick in his woven bridle,
> Of uses manifold.

Most handsomely was this man attired in green, and the hair of his head matching the horse. Fair flowing hair falls about his shoulders, a beard the size of a bush hangs over his chest which with the splendid hair which extends from his head was shorn round in a circle above his elbows, so that the halves of his arms were enveloped thereunder after the fashion of a king's hood enclosing his throat. The mane of that great horse was much like to it, well crisped and combed, with many knots plaited into it with gold thread round the bright green, ever a twist of the hair and another of gold. The tail and the topknot were similarly entwined, and both of them bound with a band of bright green, studded with precious stones as far as the dock lasted. Furthermore, there was a firm knot at the top, tied with a lace, where rang many bright bells of fire-refined gold. Such a steed, or such a man as rides him, was never beheld by eye in that hall ere that time.

> Nimble he looked as lightning,
> So every one allows;
> It seemed no mortal ever
> Might live beneath his blows.

Even so he had neither helm nor hauberk, nor pysan nor such plate as is associated with armour, nor shield nor spearshaft to thrust with and smite; but in his one hand he held a holly bunch which is greenest of hue when the groves are most bare, and in his other an axe, monstrous and huge, a battle-axe cruel to tell of, whoever might try. The head was the full length of an ell-rod, the base of the blade shaped of green steel and gold, the blade burnished bright, with a broad edge as well shaped for shearing as sharp razors are. That grim man gript it by its strong staff of a handle, which was bound round with iron to the stave's end, and all chased with green in lovely designs. A thong girt it round which was fastened at its head, and thereafter many a time looped along the haft, with costly tassels attached thereto a-plenty on bosses of bright green worked full richly. This knight makes his way inside and enters the hall, pressing towards the high dais and fearing no danger. He greeted never a one but looked high over their heads. The first word that he uttered – 'Where,' he demanded, 'is the master of this host? I would gladly set eyes on that man and hold speech with him.'

> He glared upon the knights there,
> Rolled his eyes up and down;
> He stopped and studied closely
> Who there held most renown.

There was prolonged staring to behold the man, for every one marvelled what it might mean that a knight and horse should take on such a hue as to grow green as grass, and greener it seemed, glowing brighter than green enamel on gold. All who stood there watched and drew closer to him, with all the world's wonder as to what he would do. For they had seen many marvels, but never such before, and therefore the folk there deemed it fantasy and faerye. Thus many a gallant man feared to make answer, and all were astounded at his voice and sat stonestill, in a deep silence throughout the noble hall, as though all had slipped into sleep, so suddenly were they stilled of their speech.

> I judge not all for fear,
> But some in courtesy;
> – But let him whom all obey
> Speak to that man they see.

Then Arthur beholds this adventure before the high dais and saluted him fittingly, for he was never afraid, and said, 'Sir, welcome indeed to this place. My name is Arthur, lord of this dwelling. Dismount if it please thee and stay here, I pray thee, and what thy will is we shall come to know later.' 'Nay', said the knight, 'so may He help me that sits on high, it was not my errand to stay any while in this place. But because thy praise, prince, is raised up so high, and thy stronghold and warriors are reckoned the best and stoutest to ride steel-clad on steeds, most warlike and worthiest in all the world, and doughty to play with at other fine sports, and chivalry is shown forth here, as I have heard tell – it is that which has brought me hither, i'faith, at this time. You may be assured by this branch I carry that I come in peace and seek no peril; for had I fared out in force, in fighting fashion, I have a hauberk at home and a helm too, a shield and sharp spear all shining bright, and further weapons for wielding, I vow. But because I wanted no warfare, my garments are softer. But if thou be so bold as all men reckon, thou wilt readily grant me the sport which I ask as my right.'

> Arthur made him answer,
> And said, 'Sir courteous knight,
> If thou crave naked battle,
> Thou'lt not fail here to fight.

'Nay, I seek no fight, in good faith I tell thee. Upon these benches are but beardless boys! If I were hasped in arms on a tall steed, there is none here to match me, so feeble their strength. Therefore I crave in this court a game at Christmas, for it is Yule and New Year, and many a brisk man present. If any in this household holds him so hardy, is so bold in his blood, so hot in his head, that he dare without flinching strike one blow for another, I shall give him of my gift this noble gisarme, this axe which is heavy enough, to handle as he please, and I will bide the first blow as bare as I sit here. If any knight be so fell as to try what I speak of, let him quickly leap towards me and take hold of this weapon. I renounce it for ever, let him keep it for his own, and I will stand up to his stroke unmoved on this floor – so long as thou grant me judgement to deal him another unhindered.

> 'And yet give him a respite
> A twelvemonth and a day;
> Now haste, and let see quickly
> What any here dare say.'

If he astounded them at first, stiller then were all the courtiers in hall, the high and the low. The man on his steed turned in his saddle and fiercely rolled his red eyes round, bent his bristled green-glittering brows, and swept his beard from side to side, to await who would arise. When none would hold him in talk he coughed aloud, hemmed full richly, and made ready to speak. 'What! Is this Arthur's house,' said the knight then, 'of which so much report runs through so many kingdoms? Where now are your pride and your conquests, your valiancy, your wrath, and your great words? The revel and renown of the Round Table are now overthrown with a word of one man's speech, for each cowers for fear without a blow shown!' With this he laughs so loud that the lord grieved; the blood shot for shame into his fair face and feature.

> He grew wroth as the wind,
> As did all who were there.
> The king so brave by nature
> Then stood that bold man near,

And said, 'By heaven, knight, thy request is but foolish, and since thou hast sought folly, 'tis meet thou find it. I know no man who is frightened by thy big words. Now for God's sake give me thy gisarme, and I shall grant thy boon that thou hast asked.' Quickly he leaps towards him and caught hold of his hand: then fiercely that other lights down on his feet. Now Arthur takes his axe and grips on the halve, and brandishes it grimly, like one that thought to strike therewith. The bold fellow stood towering before him, higher than any in the house by a head or more. Sternly he stroked his beard where he stood, and with an unmoved countenance turned down his tunic, no more daunted or dismayed for Arthur's great blows than if some one had brought him wine to drink on the bench.

> Gawain, who sat beside the queen,
> To the king see him incline;
> I beseech you now with unfeigned speech
> This contest might be mine.

'Honoured lord', said Gawain to the king, if you would bid me descend from this bench and stand there alongside you, so that without discourtesy I might leave this table and my liege lady be not displeased, I would come to counsel you before your high court. For to me it appears not seemly, as is held for truth, when such a request is raised so high in your hall, that you take it upon yourself, desirous of it though you be, while so many gallant men sit round you at table that there are none under heaven, to my mind, more warlike of will or better in the field where battle is joined. I am the weakest, I know, and feeblest of wit, and my life the least loss, whoever seeks truth. Only in so far as you are my uncle am I to be praised; no excellence save your blood do I know in my body. And since this business is so foolish that it does not fall to your lot, and I have asked it first of you, then grant it me, and if I speak not fairly, let all this court freely decide.

> The court took whispered counsel,
> And thereafter advised the same,
> To free the king with crown
> And give Gawain the game.

Then the king commanded the knight to rise up, and he
promptly arose and arrayed himself well, knelt down
before the king and seizes that weapon; and graciously he
relinquished it to him and lifted his hand and gave him
God's blessing, and cheerfully bids him that his heart and
hand should both be hardy. 'Take heed, cousin, said the
king, 'how thou lay on one blow, and if thou manage
him aright, I heartily believe thou shalt abide the stroke
he shall offer thereafter.' Gawain goes to the man with
gisarme in hand, and he greets him boldly, he was none
the more dismayed thereat. Then the knight in green
speaks to Sir Gawain. Let us state again our bargain, ere
we go further. First I demand of thee, knight, that thou
tell me truly what thou art called, so that I may trust to it.
'In good faith,' said the good knight, 'I am called Gawain
who offer thee this buffet, betide what may thereafter;
and this time twelvemonth will take its fellow of thee
with what weapon thou wilt, and along with no other
living soul.'

> That other returns answer,
> 'Sir Gawain, so might I thrive
> As I am wondrous fain
> That thou this blow shalt drive.

'Bigog,' said the Green Knight, 'it pleases me that I shall have at thy hand what I have sought for here. And thou hast rehearsed full and clean, with true words, the whole covenant I asked of the king, save that thou shalt assure me, man, by thy troth, that thou wilt thyself seek me out wherever thou judge I may be found on earth, and fetch thee such wages as thou wilt deal me this day before this noble company.' 'Where should I seek thee?' asked Gawain. 'Where is thy place? I know thee not, knight, thy court nor thy name. But instruct me truly thereof, and tell me how thou art called, and I shall employ all my wit to get me thither; and that I swear to thee for truth and by my honest troth.' 'That is enough at New Year, no more is needed,' said the man in green to the courteous Gawain. If I tell thee aright when I have thy blow, and thou hast smoothly smitten me, quickly tell thee of my house and home and my proper name, then thou mayest ask after me and hold to thy bargain. And if I spend no speech, then thou speedest the better, for thou canst stay at home and seek no further. But enough!

> 'Lay hold on thy grim weapon,
> Display now thy hard knocks.'
> 'Gladly, sir, believe me,'
> Said Gawain. His axe he strokes.

The Green Knight duly takes his stand, bent his head a little and discovers the flesh. His long lovely locks he laid over his crown, let the naked neck show to the short hair. Gawain gripped his axe and swings it on high, his left foot he set to ground before him. He let it light down smartly on the bare flesh, so that the knight's weapon sundered the bones and shrank through the glistening fat and shore it in twain, that the edge of the bright steel bit into the ground. The fair head fell from the neck to the floor, so that many spurned at it with their feet where it rolled forth. The blood spurted from the body, gleamed on the green, but none the more did the knight falter or fall. But un-dismayed he strode forward stiff-legged, and fiercely he reached out where the knights were standing, caught at his handsome head and straightway lifted it up, and afterwards turned towards his horse, seizes the bridle, steps into the stirrup-iron, and mounts aloft. His head he holds in his hand by the hair, and the man sat as firmly in his saddle as if no mishap ailed him, headless though he was in that place.

> He turned his trunk about,
> That ugly body that bled;
> Many a one had fear of him
> By the time his say was said.

For he held the head straight up in his hand, directed the face towards the noblest on the dais, and it lifted up its eyelids and looked all round and spoke thus much with its mouth, as you may now hear. 'Look to it, Gawain, that thou be ready to go as thou hast promised, and seek faithfully till thou find me, man, as thou hast pledged in this hall, in these knights' hearing. Make thy way to the Green Chapel, I charge thee, to fetch such a buffet as thou hast dealt out – thou hast earned it! – to be briskly repaid on New Year's morn. Many men know me: the Knight of the Green Chapel. If then thou try to find me, thou canst not fail. Come therefore, or thou must needs be called recreant.' With a savage roar he turns the reins, haled out of the door, his head in his hand, so that fire of flint flew from the steed's hooves. No one there knew to what region he betook him, any more than they knew from whence he was come. What then?

> The king there and Sir Gawain
> At the Green Man laugh and grin;
> Yet plainly was it reckoned
> A marvel amongst those men.

Though the gracious king Arthur had wonder in his heart, he let no sign of it be seen, but said aloud to the fair queen with courteous speech: 'Dear lady, be not dismayed today of all days. Such an affair becomes Christmas well, the playing of interludes, to laugh and to sing, among these seemly caroles of knights and ladies. Nevertheless, I may well address me to my meat, for I have seen a marvel, I cannot deny it.' He looked at Sir Gawain and said graciously, 'Now sir, hang up thine axe, thou hast hewn enough!' And it was placed over the dais to hang against a tapestry, that all men might behold it for a portent and with just claim tell the wonder thereof. Then they went to a table, these men together, the king and the good knight, and brave squires served them twice over with all such dainties as might be found most delightful, with all manner of meat and minstrelsy too. That day they spent in joy, till it wore to its end in the world.

> Now bethink thee well, Sir Gawain,
> That thou shrink not in dismay
> From seeking this adventure
> Thou hast ta'en in hand this day.

2

THIS EARNEST OF ADVENTURES HAD Arthur as a beginning in the New Year, for he longed to hear of lofty enterprise. Though they lacked words when the company went to be seated, they are provided now with stern work, their hands cramfull. Gawain was cheerful beginning those sports in hall, but wonder not though the end prove heavy; for though men be merry-hearted when they take strong drink, a year passes full quickly and never yields its like. Seldom the beginning accords with the end. And so this Yuletide passed away, and the year thereafter, and each season in turn followed on the other. After Christmas came the crabbed Lent which tries our flesh with fish and sparer diet. But then the world's weather contends against winter, the cold shrinks down, clouds are uplifted, the rain descends brightly in warm showers, falling on the fair plain. Flowers appear there, both meadows and groves are apparelled in green; birds make ready to build, and sing piercingly for solace of the soft summer that follows thereafter along the hillsides.

> And blossoms fill and flower
> In rows full rich and rare;
> Then noble notes a-plenty
> Are heard in forest fair.

Thereafter the season of summer with its soft winds, when
Zepherus blows gently on seeds and herbs. Most joyous is
the plant that grows therefrom, when the wetting dew
drops from the leaves to await a joyous gleam of the bright
sun. But then harvest comes hastening and hardens it
soon, warns it because of winter to wax full ripe. With
drought he drives the dust to rise and fly full high from the
face of the earth. Fierce wind from the welkin wrestles
with the sun, the leaves slip from the bough and alight on
the ground, and the grass grows grey which was green
before. Then all ripens and rots which sprang up in the
beginning, and thus the year runs into yesterday's many,
and winter winds back again, as the world (who may
doubt it?) demands.

> Till Michaelmas moon
> Was come with winter's gage;
> Then Gawain bethinks him soon
> Of his long and dreary voyage.

Even so he stays with Arthur till All-Hallows-Day. And for the knight's sake the king provided handsomely at that feast, with much rich revel of the Round Table. Courteous knights and comely ladies were heavy for love of that man, but nevertheless and none the less readily they spoke only of mirth. Many a sad heart made jests there for that gentle knight's sake. For after meat he talked sorrowfully with his uncle, spoke of his journey, and said in their hearing: 'Liege lord of my life, I now crave leave of you. You know the nature of the case; I have no desire to tell you further the trials thereof, save this little. But tomorrow morning I shall set forward without defence to the blow, to seek the Green Knight, as God will direct me.' Then the best men of the castle drew together, Ywain and Eric and many another, Sir Dodinal le Sauvage, the duke of Clarence, Lancelot and Lionel and the good Lucan, Sir Bors and Sir Bedevere, big men both, and many another nobleman along with Mador de la Port. All this press of courtiers drew nearer the king with grief at heart, to counsel the knight. There was much bitter sorrow felt in hall that a man so worshipful as Gawain must set off on that mission, to stand a dolorous blow and deal out none with his sword.

> The knight showed ever good heart,
> And said, 'What should I fear?
> What can one do but make trial
> Of destiny fair or drear?'

He remains there that day and prepares him in the morning, asks early for his arms, and they were all fetched. First a carpet of red silk of Toulouse was spread over the floor, and plenteous were the gold accoutrements that gleamed thereon. The gallant man steps on to it and handles the armour, dressed in a doublet of costly Tharsian stuff, and afterwards a cunningly-wrought hood caught up at the throat, which was lined inside with shining blaunner. Then they placed the sabatouns on the knight's feet, his legs were lapped in steel with handsome greaves, with highly burnished polaynes attached thereto and secured round his knees with knots of gold. Good cuisses thereafter which elegantly enclosed his thick and muscled thighs, with thongs tied to them; and then the woven corslet of glittering steel rings enveloped that knight over handsome stuffs; and well polished brace upon his two arms, with fine showy elbow-pieces and gloves of plate, and all the goodly gear which might avail him on that occasion.

> With a splendid cote-armure,
> His gold spurs fastened in pride;
> Girded with a trusty sword
> On a silk belt at his side.

When he was hasped in arms, how brave was his harness!
The least lachet or loop was resplendent with gold. Thus
armed as he was, he hears his Mass, offered and wor-
shipped at the high altar. Thereafter he comes to the king
and his fellows at court, lovingly takes leave of lords and
ladies, and they kissed him and brought him on his way,
commending him to Christ. By then Gringolet was ready
and girt with a saddle which gleamed bright with many
gold fringes, newly studded with nails throughout in
readiness for that adventure; the bridle barred all over and
bound with bright gold. The equipment of the paytrure
and the proud skirts, the crupper and the caparison, was of
a piece with the saddlebows; and everywhere set against
red were costly gold nails which glittered and glanced like
sunbeams. Then he takes up his helm and quickly he
kisses it; it was strengthened with clasps and padded inside.
It towered on his head and fastened behind, with a light
covering over the aventail embroidered and worked with
the finest gems on broad silken borders, and birds on the
seams, such as parrots preening between, and turtles and
true-lovers' knots onset as thick as if many a maid had
been busied thereon for seven winters.

> The circlet was yet more precious
> Which girt about his brow;
> A device it was of diamonds,
> All glittering to the show.

Then they showed him the shield, which was of bright gules, with the pentangle depicted in colours of pure gold. He seizes it by the baldric and casts it about his neck, which became that knight most handsomely. And though it delay me, it is my intention to tell you why the pentangle pertains to that prince. It is a symbol which Solomon one time appointed to betoken good faith, by the just claim it has, for it is a figure which has five points, and each line overlaps and is bound up with the other, and it is everywhere endless; and the English, so I hear, everywhere call it the Endless Knot. It therefore suits well this knight and his bright armour; for ever faithful in five things, and in each case fivefold, Gawain was acknowledged a good man, and like refined gold voided of all baseness he was graced in this world with virtues.

> Therefore the fresh pentangle
> On shield and coat he bore;
> Most faithful to his plighted word,
> And gentlest of speech and lore.

First he was found faultless in his five wits, and next the knight never failed of his five fingers, and all his trust on earth was in the five wounds which Christ suffered on the Cross, as the Creed tells. And wheresoever this man stood in battle his constant thought through all else was on this, how he derived all his strength from the five joys which Heaven's gracious Queen had of her Child. Because of this the knight had her image seemlily depicted in the larger half of his shield, so that when he glanced thereat his courage never failed. The fifth five which I find the man practised was generosity and love of his fellows above everything, his chastity and courtesy went never awry, and piety, which surpasses all other qualities: these glorious five were attached more firmly to that knight than to any other. Now all these five multiples were in truth girt to this knight, and each one joined to the other, so that no one had an end, and fixed to five points which never failed, nor ever gathered together on any side, nor sundered either; without an end at any angle wheresoever, I find, wherever the device started or came to its completion. Therefore there was royally fashioned on his gleaming shield, with red gold upon red gules, the Knot which learned folk call the pure pentangle.

> Now the gay Gawain is ready,
> He seized his lance so sure,
> And gave them all good-day,
> – He thought for evermore.

He pricked his horse with his spurs and sprang forth on his way, so briskly that sparks struck out of the stone behind him. All who saw that fair knight sighed in their hearts, and men spoke softly together one to the other, in grief for the gallant man. 'By Christ, 'tis pity thou shalt be lost, man, so noble of life as thou art! To find his peer on earth, in faith, is not easy. It were wiser to have acted more cannily, and to have made a duke of yonder dear knight. To be a shining leader of men in our land would beseem him well, and so had he better been than utterly destroyed, beheaded by an elvish man through overweening pride. Who ever knew any king to take such counsel as knights in their triflings at Christmas sport?' There was much warm water a-stream from their eyes when that glorious knight left the dwellings of men that day.

> No longer did he tarry,
> But quickly went his way;
> Many a devious route he rode,
> As I heard the book say.

This knight Sir Gawain, in God's name, rides now through the realm of Logres, though it was no pleasure to him. Many a time, friendless, he spends the night alone in a place where he did not find before him the fare he would wish. Save his steed he had no companion through woods and hills, and none save God to talk with on the way, till he drew full nigh into North Wales. All the isles of Anglesey he keeps to his left hand and traverses the fords on the foreshore, across at the Holy Head, until he again reached the shore in the wilderness of Wirral. But few dwelled there whom God or man loved with good heart. And always as he journeyed he asked of the men he met with whether they had heard any talk of a Green Knight or of the Green Chapel in any place thereabout. And all gave him no for an answer, that never in their life had they at any time seen a man of such green colouring.

> The knight took pathways strange,
> On many a dreary hill;
> Before he sees that Chapel
> His mood shall vary still.

He scaled many a cliff in regions weird, and parted far from his friends he rides a stranger. At every shore or river side where the knight passed he found a foe opposed to him, else it was wonder, and that so foul and cruel that he must needs fight him. He finds so many marvels there among the mountains that it were over-hard to tell the tenth of it. Sometimes he fights with dragons, and with wolves besides; sometimes with trolls which dwelt in the crags, with bulls and bears too, with boars at other times, and ogres which panted after him from the high fells. Had he not been hard and enduring, and were he not in God's service, doubtless he had been slain time upon time. For fighting did not so much irk him but that winter was worse, when the cold clear water shed from the clouds and froze ere it might fall to the dark earth. Nigh slain with the sleet, he slept in steel more nights than enough, among the naked rocks, where the cold brook runs clattering from the crest and hung high over his head in hard icicles. Thus rides this knight through the land, in peril and pain and grievous plights, alone until Christmas eve.

> The knight at that season
> To Mary made his plea,
> That she might yet appoint him
> Some shelter, there to be.

In the morning he rides merrily past a mountain into a deep forest which was wondrous wild, high hills on every side and holtwoods thereunder of huge hoary oaks, a hundred together. The hazel and hawthorn were fast entwined, with rough frosty moss draped everywhere, and on the bare branches many joyless birds which piped there piteously for pain of the cold. The knight on Gringolet slips beneath them through many a swamp and mire, a man all alone, anxious for his affairs, lest he should not contrive to see the service of that Lord who that selfsame night was born of a maiden, our strife to quell. And so he said, sighing, 'Lord, I beseech thee, and Mary that gentlest mother so dear, that I might hear Mass devoutly at some refuge, and Thy Matins ill the morning. Meekly I ask it, and quickly to that end I pray my pater and ave and creed.'

> He rode while he was praying,
> Cried out for each misdeed,
> Signed himself time and time again,
> And said, 'Christ's Cross me speed!'

He had signed himself, this knight, but thrice ere he was aware in the wood of a dwelling within a moat, above a clearing, on a mound, framed under the boughs of many a massive tree-trunk round about its dykes. A castle the comeliest that ever knight possessed, pitched on a meadow with a park all round, with a palisade of stakes set closely together for more than two miles, surrounding many a tree. The knight contemplated that stronghold from one side as it shimmered and shone through the shining oaks. Then courteously he doffed his helm and devoutly thanks Jesus and Saint Julian, who are gentle both, that they had shown him courtesy and hearkened to his cry. 'Now good lodging, cried the knight, 'I beseech of you yet!' Then he pricks Gringolet with his golden heels, and quite by chance has struck upon the main road, which brought the man briskly to the drawbridge end.

> The bridge was pulled up firmly,
> The gates secured fast,
> The walls were in brave order,
> It feared no tempest's blast.

The knight, tarrying on his steed, waited on the bank of the deep double moat which hemmed the place in. The wall sank wondrous deep into the water and further towered aloft a full great height of hard hewn stone as far as the cornice, fortified under the battlements after the best fashion; and thereafter gay watchtowers set at intervals with many a fair loophole which fastened right clean. A better barbican the knight never beheld, and further within he might observe the lofty hall, towers erected now here, now there, and thickly pinnacled, and fair matching turrets, wondrously long, with carved tops most cunningly made. Chalkwhite chimneys he observed there in plenty over the tower roofs, gleaming so whitely. So many painted pinnacles were powdered everywhere, clustered so thick among the castle's embrasures, that verily it looked as though pared out of paper. To the gallant man on his steed it seemed fair prospect enough if he might contrive to come inside the enclosure to lodge pleasantly in that hostel while the Holy Day lasted.

> He called, and soon there came
> A porter mighty pleasant;
> He heard his errand from the wall,
> And greeted the knight errant.

'Good sir', said Gawain, 'wouldst go mine errand to the noble lord of this household, to ask for lodging?' 'Yea, by Saint Peter,' quoth the porter, and truly I believe that you are welcome, sir, to stay as long as it please you.' Then the porter returned straightway, and folk with him honourably, to receive the knight. They let down the great drawbridge and came courteously out, and knelt down on their knees on the cold earth to give this same knight such welcome as they deemed worthy. They made him free of the broad gate, set back wide, and he raised them graciously and rode across the bridge. Divers folk held to his saddle while he alighted, and thereafter brave men a-plenty stabled his steed. Knights and squires then came down to bring this warrior joyously into hall. When he lifted his helm, men enough hastened to take it from his hands and serve the gracious lord. They took his sword and his shield both. Then he saluted each of the knights full graciously, and many a proud one pressed forward to honour that prince. Decked in his fine array, they led him to the hall, where a good fire burned fiercely on the hearth. Then the lord of that household comes out from his chamber to meet in all courtesy the man in hall. 'You are welcome,' he said, 'to be here as you please. Everything that is here, it is all your own, to have at your pleasure and dispose of.'

> 'I thank you,' said Sir Gawain,
> 'And Christ make good your grace!'
> Each knew joy of the other,
> Folded in close embrace.

Gawain looked on the man who had given him such fair greeting, and it seemed to him the stronghold had a doughty master. A huge man in the prime of life, his beard was broad and bright and reddish-brown; formidable, firmly poised on stalwart legs, his face fell as fire and his speech gallant, in truth it well became him, Sir Gawain thought, to be lord of a worthy company in a castle. The lord turned to a chamber and particularly commands that they appoint Sir Gawain a servant to wait on him with reverence; and at his bidding there were men enough ready who brought him to a handsome chamber where the bedding was noble, bed-hangings of bright silk with clear gold hems and curious coverlets with lovely panels, gay blaunner on the surface worked round about, curtains running on cords with red gold rings, tapestries of stuff of Toulouse and Tharsia hung on the wall, and the same underfoot on the chamber floor. There amidst merry talk the knight was stripped of his mail shirt and his bright garments. Servitors promptly fetched him rich robes to put on and change into and choose which he thought best. As soon as he had taken one and was clad therein, which sat on him fairly with flowing skirts, verily to well-nigh every one it seemed the springtide in all its colours, his limbs under it glowing and lovely, so that Christ as they thought never made handsomer knight.

> Whence ever he had come to them,
> It seemed in truth he might
> Be prince without a peer
> In field where fell men fight.

A chair with its coverings was duly set for Sir Gawain before the fireside where charcoal burned, and cushions upon quilted work which were both cunningly made; and then a gay mantle was placed on the knight of a brown bleant, richly embroidered and well lined inside with the best fur, adorned with ermine, and his hood the same. And he sat down in that handsome seat and quickly warmed himself, and with that his mood grew gayer.

Straightway a table was set up on goodly trestles and covered with a clean cloth shining clear and white, with napkins and salt cellars and silver spoons. The man washed at his will and went to his meat. Attendants gave him seemly service enough, with divers proper broths seasoned of the best, twofold as is fitting, and many kinds of fish, some baked in bread, some grilled on the coals, some boiled, some savoured in stews with spices, and always such cunning sauces as pleased the knight. Oft times the gallant man most kindly and graciously called it a feast, when the attendants courteously exhorted him together:

> 'Take now this meatless penance,
> It shall later be amended.'
> The knight laughed and grew merry,
> As wine to his head ascended.

Then there was tactful search and inquiry put to the prince himself by discreet questioning, so that he courteously acknowledged he was of that court which the noble Arthur rules alone, who is the glorious royal king of the Round Table, and that it was Gawain himself who sits in that dwelling, come for those Christmas celebrations as chance had then befallen him. When the lord had learned that he had that knight, he laughed aloud thereat, such a pleasure he thought it; and all the men in the castle were then delighted to appear promptly before him to whose person pertains all excellence and prowess and refined virtues, and who is praised ever. His honour is greatest above all men alive. Every one said quietly to his fellow: 'We shall now see the refinements of good manners at their best, and faultless figures of noble speech. We may learn unasked what is profitable in discourse, since we have taken among us that fine father of nurture. Truly, God has granted us His grace in full measure, who permits us to have such a guest as Gawain when men for joy of Christ's birth shall sit and sing.

> 'To the heart of noble manners
> This man will help us reach;
> I trow that they who hear him
> Shall learn true lovers' speech.'

By the time dinner was done and the knight risen the hour had drawn near to nightfall. Priests made their way to the chapels, rang full nobly, as they were bound, to the devout evensong of that high festival. The lord turns thereto, the lady also, who enters gracefully a handsome closet. Gawain hastens gaily and forthwith goes thither. The lord takes him by the fold of his gown and leads him to where he shall sit, familiarly acknowledges him and calls him by name, and said he was the most welcome of men upon earth. And Gawain thanked him warmly, and each saluted the other, and they sat gravely together during the service. Then the lady was minded to look on the knight; she came forth from her closet with many sweet maidens. She was the fairest favoured in flesh and fell, in proportion and colour and manner, of all women else, and lovelier than Guenevere, so Sir Gawain thought. He strode through the chancel to cherish that beauty. A second lady led her by the left hand, who was older than she, a beldame it seemed, and highly honoured with squires about her. But those ladies were unlike to look on, for if the young one was fresh, the other was withered; rich red on the one was arrayed everywhere, rough wrinkled cheeks hung in folds on the other. Kerchiefs on the one, with many clear pearls; her breast and bright throat displayed all bare shone sheerer than snow which falls on the hills. The other was swathed about the neck with a gorger, bound over her dark chin with chalkwhite veils; her forehead enfolded in silk, muffled all over, and turreted and trellised about with trefoils. There was naught naked of that lady save the black brows, two eyes and the nose, the bare lips – and those were sour to see and wondrous bleared. A worshipful dame of this world one may call her, God knows!

> Her body was short and thick,
> Her buttocks bayed and wide;
> Far sweeter to man's taste
> Was the lady at her side.

When Gawain beheld that gay lady who looked so graciously, with leave gained of the lord he went to meet with them. He saluted the elder, bowing full low; the younger he enfolded somewhat in his arms; he kisses her sweetly and speaks like true knight. They crave his acquaintance, and forthwith he asks to be their leal servant, if it so pleased them. They set him between them, and with talk they conduct him to the chamber, to the fireplace, and in especial they ask for spices, which men hastened to bring without stint, and each time pleasant wine therewith. The lord courteously gets to his feet, many a time bade that mirth should be kindled, merrily doffed his hood and hung it from a spear and waved it at them to win the glory thereof, so that all possible mirth might be roused that Christmastide. 'And I shall try, by my faith, to contend with the best ere I lack this garment with the help of my friends!' Thus with laughing words the lord makes things merry, to cheer Sir Gawain with sport in hall that night.

> Until the time was on them
> The lord commanded light;
> Then Sir Gawain took his leave,
> And to his bed him dight.

In the morning, as each man minds the time that Our Lord was born to die for our destiny, joy breeds in every one a delight in the world for His sake. So did it there that day through much handsome faring. Both at mess and at meal brave men served on the dais rare dishes of the best. The ancient beldame she sits highest; the lord gallantly took place next to her, that I know. Gawain and the gay lady sat together right in the midst as the dishes came duly; and thereafter each throughout the hall, as was held best, to each man in his degree there was fair service. There was meat, there was mirth, much joy was there, to tell of which were a trial to me if perchance I troubled to recount it in detail. But yet I know that Gawain and that sweet lady found such solace in their company together, through the dear courtly converse of their private speech, with clean courteous talk free from stain, that in truth their sport surpassed the play of princes.

> With trumpets and side drums,
> Much piping there repairs;
> Each man minded his business,
> And they two minded theirs.

Much merriment they made there that day and the next, and the third came in quite as crowded thereafter. The joy of St John's day was noble to hear, and was the festival's end, the folk there thought. There were guests to depart in the grey morning, so marvellously they stayed awake and drank wine, danced unceasing their fair caroles. At last, when it was late, they took their leave, each gallant man to go on his way. Gawain said goodbye, but the good man takes hold of him, leads him to his own chamber beside the fireplace, and there he holds him back and thanks him courteously for the fine favour he had shown them in honouring his home over that festival and embellishing his castle with his gracious presence. 'Indeed, sir, so long as I live it will be the better for me that Gawain has been my guest on God's own feast.' 'I thank you, sir,' said Gawain, 'but in good faith it is yours, all the honour is your own, the King on high repay you! And I am at your command, to do your bidding in great things and small, as I am rightly beholden.'

> The lord was at great pains
> To hold longer the knight
> To him Gawain answers,
> That in no way he might.

Then the lord questioned him courteously what compelling deed had driven him at that festival time to wander from the king's court so daringly alone, ere the holy days were wholly passed from the dwellings of men. 'Indeed, sir,' said the knight, 'you speak but truth. A high and pressing errand fetched me from those precincts, for I find myself summoned to seek out a place I know not where in the world to turn to find it. I had rather than all the land in Logres I might come upon it on New Year's morn, so help me our Lord! And so, sir, I make this request of you here, that you tell me truly if ever you heard tell of the Green Chapel, where it stands on earth, and of the knight green of colour that keeps it. A tryst was made by covenant between us to meet that man at that very place, if I should live; and of that same New Year it now lacks but little. By God's sun, gladlier would I look on that man, would God permit it, than possess any good thing. Therefore, indeed, with your leave I must needs be on my way. I have now but a bare three days to act in, and I had as soon fall dead as fail of my errand.' Then said the lord, laughing: 'Now you must needs stay longer!' For I shall direct you to that meeting-place by your term's end. Let the Green Chapel grieve you no more, where it stands, but you shall be in your bed, good sir, till well into the day, and set out on the first of the year and come to that meeting-place at mid-morning, to do what business you please there.

> 'Rise then and set off briskly,
> But stay till New Year's day
> It is not two miles distant,
> We shall set you in the way.'

Then Gawain was delighted and laughed merrily. 'Now above all else I thank you heartily. Now that my adventure is accomplished, I shall remain at your wish and do what else you determine.' With that the lord caught hold of him and sat beside him; he had the ladies fetched to please them the better. There was pleasant entertainment among themselves apart, and the lord for affection spoke words as merry as one who would take leave of his senses or knew not what he would. Then he spoke to the knight, calling out aloud: 'You have determined to do the deed which I ask. Will you hold to your promise here and now?' 'Aye, sir, truly,' said that true knight, 'so long as I am in your castle I will be obedient to your command.' 'Because you have had a sore journey,' said the lord, 'and travelled from afar, and since you have kept awake with me, you are not well furnished either with sustenance or sleep, I know it well. You must stay in your upper chamber and lie on at your ease tomorrow till the hour of Mass, and go to meat when you will with my wife, who shall sit with you and entertain you with her company till I return to court. Do you remain so,

> 'And I shall rise up early,
> A-hunting will I go.'
> Gawain grants all this to him,
> A true knight, bowing low.

'Still further,' said the lord, 'let us make a bargain. Whatsoever I win in the forest shall become yours, and what advantage you achieve do you exchange with me in return. Sweet sir, let us swap so! Answer truly, knight, whether better or worse betide.' 'By God,' said the good Gawain, 'I agree to that, and I am happy that you are pleased to make sport.' 'Who brings us this drink? The bargain is made!' said the lord of that people. They laughed each one, they drank and trifled and revelled light-heartedly, these lords and ladies, for as long as they pleased. And afterwards with polite behaviour and many fair words they stood up and made an end, and spoke quietly and kissed graciously and took their leave. With many a nimble servant and with gleaming torches each man was brought at last to his bed, full soft.

> Yet ere they made off bedwards,
> They checked their bargain oft;
> The old lord of that people
> Could well keep sport aloft.

3

LONG BEFORE DAY PEOPLE WERE RISING. Guests who must depart called their servants and they rose up briskly to saddle the horses; they make ready their gear and truss their bags, apparel them most handsomely to ride in fine array, mount up quickly and seize their bridles, each man on his way wherever he pleased. The dear lord of the land was not the last dressed for riding, and many companions with him. Quickly he ate a sop when he had heard Mass, and makes haste with bugle to the hunting field. By the time any daylight gleamed over the earth, he and his squires were on their tall steeds. Then these knowing dog-grooms coupled their hounds, unfastened the kennel door and called them outside, blew loudly on their bugles three long notes. At that the hounds barked and made fierce din; and they whipped and turned back those that went chasing, a hundred choice huntsmen, as I have heard tell.

> The keepers went to stations,
> Huntsmen unleashed the hounds,
> Loud uproar filled the forest
> When each his great horn sounds.

The wild things trembled at the first note of the baying. Deer rushed to the valley, doting for fear, or climbed to the high ground, but were briskly driven back by the beaters' ring, who loudly shouted. The harts with towering heads they let pass, the brave bucks too with their broad antlers, for that noble lord had forbidden that any should harass the male deer in the close season. The hinds were kept back with a *hey*! and a *war*! the does driven with uproar to the deep valleys. There might one see the glancing of arrows as they were loosed, at each turn in the forest a shaft flashed forth, which bit fiercely on brown hides with their broad heads. What! they bray and they bleed, they die on the hillsides, and ever the dashing dogs pursue them close, and hunters hastened after them with their loud horns, with such ringing noise as if the cliffs had shattered. By the time they had been harassed on the high ground and driven to the water, whatever creature escaped the men who were shooting was seized and rent at the receiving stations. The men at the lower stations were so skilled, and the greyhounds so huge which seized them in an instant and dragged them down there, as fast as the men might run up.

> The lord was transported with joy,
> Full oft would race and alight,
> And spent that day in mirth
> Thus till the dark night.

Thus, this lord disports himself along the forest's eaves, and that good man Gawain lies in a gay bed, stays hidden till daylight gleamed on the walls, under his bright coverlet and curtains drawn round. And as he dozed gently on he heard a cautious little noise at his door and heard it stealthily open. He lifts his head from under the bedclothes and caught up a corner of the curtain a little and watches warily in that direction, what it might be. It was the lady, so lovely to see, who drew the door to behind her secretly and silently and made towards the bed. The knight was embarrassed and adroitly laid him down and pretended to be asleep. She stepped silently on and stole to his bed, raised up the curtain and crept inside and sat down gently on the bedside and stayed there a wondrous long time to spy when he would awake. A long time too the knight lay lurking, debating in mind what that case might result in or mean. A strange business he thought it, yet still he said to himself, 'It were more seemly quickly to discover by my questions what she would have.' He then awoke and stretched himself and turned towards her, and opened his lids and acted like a man in amaze, and crossed himself, as though to be the safer for his prayer.

> Her chin and cheek so sweet
> With mingled white and red,
> With delicate laughing lips
> Most lovingly she said:

'Good morrow, Sir Gawain,' said that gay lady. 'How heedless a sleeper you are that one may creep hither! You are caught now, in a trice! But let us make a treaty. I shall confine you to your bed, you can rely on that!' Laughing, the lady uttered those merry words. 'Good morrow, sweet lady,' said the blithe Gawain. 'Let there be done with me as you will, for that pleases me well. For I yield at once and sue for favour – and in my judgment, since I needs must, that is the best course for me.' And thus he jested in return, with much happy laughter. 'But, lovely lady, if you would grant me leave and release your prisoner and bid him rise, I would get up from this bed and sort myself better. I should find more pleasure then in talking with you.' 'Nay truly, fair sir', said that sweet one, 'you shall not rise from your bed. I have a better plan for you. I shall enfold you here on the other side too, and afterwards talk with my knight whom I have caught. For I know well, in faith, that you are Sir Gawain, whom all the world honours wherever you ride. Your honour and courtesy are nobly praised by lords and ladies and all folk alive. And now in faith you are here, and we two on our own. My lord and his followers are gone far off, other men are in their beds, and my maidens likewise, the door drawn to and secured with a stout hasp. And since I have here in this house him who brings pleasure to all, I shall, so long as it lasts, spend my time profitably in talk.

> 'You are welcome to my body,
> Take what pleasure you will
> I needs must be your servant,
> Compulsion holds me still.'

'In good faith,' said Sir Gawain, 'I find it a good thing I am not he you now speak of. I am a man unworthy to attain to such honour as you describe, I know it only too well. By God I were happy, if it seemed good to you, might I fare with word or deed to please your excellence. That were pure joy!' 'In good faith, Sir Gawain,' said the gay lady, 'the value and prowess that pleases every one else, it were little good breeding if I found fault with it or esteemed it lightly. But there are ladies a-plenty who would rather have you in their keeping, sir, as I have you here, lovingly to disport them with your charming words, to win themselves solace and cool their cares, than much of the treasure and gold which they own. But I praise that same Lord who rules on high that by His favour I have wholly in my hand what every one desires.'

> She made him much good cheer,
> That lady so fair of face;
> The knight with unstained words
> Found answer in every case.

'Madam', said the gay man, 'may Mary repay you, for in good faith I have found in you a noble generosity. Some folk get from others full much according to their deeds, but the favour they show me is not for my deserts. It is your own worthiness, you who can do only what is well.' 'By Mary,' said that noble lady, 'it seems otherwise to me. For were I worth all the host of women alive, and all the world's wealth were in my hand, and I were to chaffer and choose to get me a husband, because of the qualities I have here found in you, sir, of beauty and courtesy and handsome demeanour, and what I have heard earlier and now consider to be true – no man on earth should be chosen before you.' 'Assuredly, dear lady,' said the knight, 'you have chosen far better. But I am proud of the esteem you hold me in, and in all seriousness your servant I hold you my sovereign, and I become your knight, and may Christ repay you.' Thus they spoke of this and that till past mid-morning, and ever the lady behaved as though she loved him greatly. The knight was on his guard and bore himself well. Though she were the fairest of women, the knight was thinking, the less love would he bring with him, by reason of the harm he sought without respite,

> The blow which must destroy him,
> And it must needs be done.
> The lady then spoke of taking leave;
> He granted it full soon.

She then gave him good-day and, glancing at him, laughed; and as she stood up she astonished him with her forbidding words. 'Now He who prospers every speech reward you for this entertainment. But that you are Gawain I find it hard to believe.' 'Why?' asked the knight, and he asked quickly, fearing lest he had come short in decorum of manner. But the lady blessed him and spoke after this fashion: 'So good a man as Gawain is properly held, and courtesy so very much part of him, might not easily have remained so long with a lady unless he had craved a kiss in courtesy, by some trifling hint at some break in the talk.' Then said Gawain, 'In truth, it shall be as you please. I shall kiss at your behest, as behoves a knight, and, for a further reason, lest you be offended. So urge it no further.' With that she comes nearer and takes him in her arms, bends lovingly down and kisses the knight. Each graciously commends the other to Christ, and she goes out at the door without further word. And he makes ready to rise and is in haste; he summons his chamberlain and chooses his garments, and when he was ready goes forth to Mass. Thereafter he went to meat, which busied him worthily, and he made merry all day till the moon rose.

> No man had warmer welcome
> From two such noble dames,
> The elder and the younger;
> Solace each gives and claims.

All this time the lord of that land has gone about his sport, hunting the barren hinds in forest and heathland. By the time the sun slanted he had slain such a number of does and other deer that it was a marvel to think of. Then at last the folk rapidly assembled and soon made a quarry of the slain deer. Those highest of rank came up with attendants a–plenty, gathered together the fattest beasts there and had them opened skilfully as the task demands. Some who were there searched them at the assay: on the worst conditioned of all they found two fingers' width. Afterwards they slit open the slot, took hold of the erber, sliced with a sharp knife and cut out the intestines. After that they chopped off the four legs and stripped away the hide; then they broke open the belly and drew out the bowels carefully, for fear of loosening the knot's ligature. They seized hold of the throat, deftly parted the gullet from the windpipe, and pulled out the guts. Then they carved out the shoulders with their sharp knives, drew them away by means of a small hole to have the sides intact. Afterwards they opened the breast, splitting it in two, and again they begin at the throat and quickly rive it right to the fork, empty out the avanters, and faithfully thereafter they cut away all the membranes along the ribs. Likewise, as is fitting, they clear along the backbone straight down to the haunch, which hung all together, and they raise it up entire and hew it off there. And that rightly, as I believe, they reckon the numbles so-called.

> By the forks of the thighs
> They loosen the folds behind;
> They hasten to hew all in twain,
> Along the backbone to unbind.

Then they hew off both head and neck, and afterwards quickly sunder the sides from the chine, and the raven's fee they flung into a thicket. Then each man for his reward, even as it falls to him to take, they pierced each stout side through at the rib and hung them up by the hocks of the legs. Upon a fair deerskin they feed their hounds with liver and lights and tripes, and bread soaked in blood mixed therewith. Staunchly they sounded the kill, and the hounds bayed. Afterwards they took up their meat and proceeded homewards, blowing loudly many a long clear note. By the time daylight was ended the company had reached that fair castle where the knight remains unperturbed.

> With joy and bright fire kindled,
> The lord comes home again;
> When he and Gawain met there,
> What mirth between the twain!

Then the lord bade assemble all the household in hall and both the ladies to come downstairs with their maidens into the presence of every one there. He commands his men diligently to fetch his venison before him, and joyously he called to Gawain, shows him the tails of those nimble beasts, points out the bright fat cut into on the ribs. 'How does this sport please you? Have I earned praise? Do I deserve warm thanks for my skill?' 'Indeed, yes,' said the other, 'here is the fairest hunting I have seen of a wintertime these seven years.' 'And I give it all to you, Gawain,' said the lord then, 'for by the terms of our agreement you may claim it all as your own.' 'That is true,' said the knight, 'and I say as much to you. What I have fairly come by within this dwelling, it shall become yours indeed, with as good a will.' He embraced his fair neck within his arms and kisses him as handsomely as he knew how. 'Take here my winnings. I found no other. I would freely grant it you in full, though it were more.' 'It is good,' said that worthy lord, 'and I thank you. It may be such that it is the better ware, if you would tell me where you won this same wealth by your wit.' 'That was not the bargain,' said he. 'Ask me no further! For you have received what is due to you. Rest assured you may have nothing more.'

> They laughed and made them merry
> With words which all can praise;
> Soon they went in to supper,
> Rare foods their spirits raise.

And afterwards they sat in a chamber by the fireside. Men fetched them choice wine often, and once again in their jesting they agreed to fulfil on the morrow the same bargain they had made before: whatever luck befell, to exchange when they met at night their winnings and whatever they gained anew. They came to this agreement before all the court, and the pledging cup was merrily brought forward for the occasion, and then at last affectionately they took their leave and each man went straightway to his bed. By the time the cock had crowed and cackled but thrice the lord had leapt from his bed, and all his servants, so that meat and Mass were duly disposed of. The company made way to the wood, to hunt, ere any day broke.

> They traversed the level country,
> Shrilly with hunt and horns;
> The dogs race headlong forward,
> Uncoupled through the thorns.

At once they call for a search by the side of a marsh. The huntsman cheered on the hounds that first let them know of it, threw fierce words at them with furious accent. Those hounds that heard this hastened there quickly and fell as fast to the trail, forty together. With that there arose such a babel and babble of assembled dogs that the cliffs rang round about. Hunters emboldened them with horn and with mouth. Then they rushed together in a pack between a pool in that wood and a frightening crag; with the men behind them, they dashed to the finding in a hillock by a cliff on the marsh's edge, where the rough rock had tumbled pell-mell. The men cast about the crag and the hillock too, till they were sure that the creature bayed by the bloodhounds was there within. Then they beat on the bushes and bade him rise up, and calamitously he made out at the men athwart his path. The most wondrous boar swung out there. Long since had that singler aged from the herd, for he was savage, the hugest of all boars. When he grunted so grimly, many were grieved; for at the first thrust he dashed three to the earth, then sprang forth at good speed without more harm done. The others halloed *hi*! full loud, and *heyl hey*! they shouted, set horn to mouth, quickly blew the recall. Many a merry outcry was there of men and dogs who make haste after this boar to slay him with clamour and din.

> He stands at bay full often,
> And maims the pack in fight;
> He injures many a hound, and they
> Run squealing for pain and fright.

Men thrust forward to shoot at him. They loosed their arrows at him, hit him often. But the points failed against the tough skin massed on his shoulders, nor would the barbs bite on his brows, though the smooth-shaven shaft shivered to pieces. The tip sprang back wherever it hit. But when the blows hurt him with their shrewd strokes, then, mad for fight, he rushes out against the men, fiercely maltreats them where he sallies forth; and many felt fear thereat and drew back anxiously. But the lord pursues him on his game steed and blows his bugle like a brave huntsman. He sounded the recall and rode through the woods pursuing this wild boar till the sun shafted. They spend the day over their deed in this wise, while our gallant knight Gawain lies happily a-bed at home, under bedclothes full richly hued.

> The lady, not forgetting,
> Came to greet him for her part;
> Full early she was at him,
> Seeking a change of heart.

She comes to the curtain and peeps in at the knight. Sir Gawain is the first to give her courteous welcome, but she readily returns him words of greeting, sits down gently at his side and laughs long, and with an affectionate glance addressed these words to him. 'Sir, if you are Gawain, a wonder it seems to me. A man who is always so strongly inclined to good, and yet knows not how to recognise the manners of good company – and if any one instructs you how to know them, you cast them from your mind. Thou hast quickly forgotten what I taught yesterday by the truest token of speech that I knew.' 'What is that?' asked the knight. 'Assuredly I knew nothing of it. If you speak truth, the blame is all mine.' 'Yet I instructed you in kissing,' said the lovely lady then, 'wherever favour is known, quickly to make your claim. That befits each knight that practises chivalry.' 'Enough of such talk, my dear lady,' said that valiant man; 'for I durst not do that, lest I were refused. If I were denied, then indeed I were wrong if I offered.' 'By my faith', said the merry lady, 'you are not to be denied. You are strong enough to constrain with force, should you wish it, if any were so ill-bred as to forbid you.' 'Ah, by God,' said Gawain, 'what you say is well enough, but compulsion is ignoble in the land where I dwell, and each gift which is not given with good will. I am at your command, to kiss when you please. You may take when you will, and when you think fit straightway leave off.'

> The lady then bends over
> And fairly kisses his face;
> Much talk they hold together
> Of true love's grief and grace.

'I would know of you, sir,' said there that noble lady, 'if it would not offend you, what might the reason be, that so young and mettlesome as you now are, so courteous and knightly as you are acknowledged far and wide – and to make choice of all chivalry, the chief thing praised is the true sport of love, the very doctrine of arms; for to tell of the labours of these true knights, it is the inscribed title and text of their deeds how men for their true love have adventured their lives, endured for their passion doleful times, and afterwards by their valour avenged and voided their care and brought bliss into bower by their own excellence. And you are acknowledged the noblest knight of your age, your fame and honour are spread everywhere, and I have sat by you here on two separate occasions, yet I have never heard one word come from your mouth which had aught to do with love, neither less nor more. And you, who are so courteous and skilled in your vows, ought readily to show and teach a young thing some tokens of the art of true love. Why! are you unlearned, you who enjoy all this praise? Or else you judge me too stupid to listen to your courtly love-talk. For shame!

> 'To learn from you such pastime,
> Unattended have I come;
> Now teach me what you know of love,
> While my lord is far from home.'

'In good faith,' declared Gawain, 'may God repay you! My joy is great and my pleasure immense that one so noble as you should make her way hither and take pains with so poor a man as to entertain your knight with any kind of favour. It is a solace to me. But to take on me the task of expounding true love and to touch on the themes of romances and knightly deeds, to you who as I well know have more skill by half in that art than a hundred such as I am or ever shall be in my life – on my word, dear lady, that were a manifold folly. I would do your will to the best of my power, as I am deeply obliged, and I will evermore be your servant, so may God save me.' Thus that noble lady put him to trial and tested him often, to have won him to sin, whatever else she was thinking. But he made so good a defence that no fault might be found, nor no evil on either side, nor knew they aught but happiness.

> Long they laughed and sported,
> She kissed him at the last;
> With that she took a gracious leave,
> And on her way she passed.

Then the knight bestirs himself and rises for Mass, and thereafter their dinner was made ready and served handsomely. The man spent the whole day pleasantly with the ladies, but the lord was many a time galloping over the countryside. He follows this dreadful boar who dashes by the hillsides and bit asunder the backs of his best dogs where he stood at bay, till the bowmen broke it and made him move on in his own despite, so many arrows sped there when the hunters assembled. Even so he made the bravest start at times, till in the end he was so exhausted he could run no more. But with such speed as he might he escapes to a hole in a mound by a rock where runs a brook. He got the bank at his back; he begins to scrape, froth foamed monstrously at the corners of his mouth, and he whets his white tusks. It was hard then for all the bold men who stood about him to harm him from a distance, but none durst draw near him for danger.

> He had hurt so many already,
> That all were then full loth
> To be torn again with his tusks,
> Who was fierce and frantic both.

Till the knight himself came, urging on his steed. He sees him standing at bay, his men round about. Nimbly he dismounts and leaves his horse, plucks out his bright sword and goes forward stoutly. He hastens through the ford where the beast is waiting. The animal was aware of the man with his weapon in hand. He set his hair a-bristling; he snorted so fiercely that many were afraid for the man, lest he get the worse of it. The boar sallies out straight at the knight, so that man and boar were the two of them in heaps in the fiercest of the water. But the other had the worse, for the man marks him well when first they encountered, set his point unflinchingly right in his breast-hollow and hit him up to the hilt, so that the heart was split, and he gave up his life snarling and went swiftly downstream.

> A hundred hounds they seized him,
> Who fiercely worry and bite;
> Men brought him to the bank,
> And the dogs to death endite.

The kill was sounded on many a fierce horn; there was high halloing aloud by those men who might. The hounds bayed that beast as their masters bade them, who were the chief hunters of that arduous chase. Then a man who was skilled in forest crafts began dexterously to unlace this boar. First he hews off his head and hangs it on high, and afterwards rends him roughly along the backbone, plucks out the bowels and broils them on the coals, and mixed with bread rewards his hounds therewith. Thereafter he cuts away the brawns in broad glistening slabs, and lifts out the entrails as is proper; and further fastens the halves all whole together and thereafter hangs them firmly on a stout pole. And now they press homewards with this same swine. The boar's head was carried before that selfsame man who slew him in the ford by force of his own strong hand.

> Until he sees Sir Gawain
> In hall he thought it long;
> He called, and he came promptly
> – Those fees to him belong.

The lord with his loud voice laughed merrily when he saw Sir Gawain; he speaks gaily. The good ladies were fetched and the household assembled. He shows them the shields of meat and shapes them a tale of the bulk and the length, the fierceness too of the wild boar's defence in the wood where he fled. The other knight courteously commended his deed, and praised it as a great proof of excellence; for such a brawn of a beast, or such sides of a boar, he had never seen before. Then they handled the huge head; the gracious knight praised it and professed horror thereat, to flatter the lord. 'Now, Gawain,' declared his host, 'this game is your own, by firm and perfect bargain, as you truly know.' 'So it is,' said the knight, 'and on my word just as surely I shall give to you in return all my winnings.' He took the lord about the neck and kisses him graciously, and immediately after he treated him there the same way. 'Now', declared the knight, 'we are even this eventide of all the covenants we knit by law since I came hither.'

> The lord said to him, 'By Saint Giles,
> You are the best I know!
> You will be rich in no time
> If you drive your bargain so.'

Then they erected tables upon trestles, and cast cloths
thereon. Clear lights were lit along the walls, and waxen
torches. Servants set the tables and waited thereat
throughout the hall. Much mirth and merry din arose
there round the hall fire, and in divers ways during and
after supper many noble songs, such as Christmas carols
and new dances, with all the seemly mirth one may tell of.
And ever our gallant knight was at the lady's side. Such
kind attention she showed him, with secret stolen glances
of favour to please the knight, that he was filled with
wonder and angry with himself; but of his courtesy he
would not meet her advances, yet treated her delightfully,
however the deed went awry.

> When they had played in hall there,
> Until their wish was spent,
> He called them to the chamber,
> And towards the fire they went.

And there they drank and discoursed and thought fit once again to propose the same terms on New Year's Eve. But the knight asked leave to depart in the morning, for it was near to the time when he must away. The lord dissuaded him therefrom, urged him to stay, and said, 'As I am true knight, I pledge my troth thou shalt come to the Green Chapel to do thine errand, sir, on New Year's morn, long before prime. Therefore lie in thy upper chamber and take thine ease, and I shall hunt in the forest and keep my bargain to exchange winnings with thee, when I have returned hither. For I have twice made trial of thee, and I find thee true. Now think in the morning, "The third time pays for all!" Let us make merry while we may and set our hearts upon joy, for a man may find sorrow whenever he wishes.' This was readily agreed to, and Gawain is stayed. Wine was brought them gaily, and they went to their beds with light.

> Sir Gawain lies there sleeping,
> Full still and soft all night;
> The lord, who follows his own ends,
> Was ready at morning light.

After Mass he and his men ate a morsel. The morning was a merry one; he asks for his mount. All the men who were to follow him on horseback were mounted ready on their steeds before the hall gates. Wondrous fair was the earth, for the frost was clinging to it. Fiery and red the sun rises over the wrack and casts the clouds clear of the welkin. The hunters unleashed at the side of a wood; the rocks rang amid the thickets for the din of their horns. Some fell in the scent where the fox awaited, trail from side to side in the practice of their wiles. A kenet announces it; the huntsman calls to him; his companions fall in on him as he sniffs full hard, and they run forth in a rabble dead in his track. And he scampers ahead of them. Forthwith they found him, and when they beheld him with their eyes they pursued him close, denouncing him knowingly with a fierce noise. And he dodges and doubles through many a tiresome grove, winds back and listens along the hedges full often. At last he leaps over a thickset hedge by a little ditch, steals out stealthily by the edge of a marshy thicket, and thought to have slipt from the wood, cunningly away from the hounds. Then, before he knew it, he had come to a well-chosen station, where three fierce grey ones menaced him at once with a rush.

> He started back as quickly,
> And staunchly swung aside;
> With all the woe in the world
> He turned to the wood to hide.

Then was it brave sport to hear the hounds, when all the pack had met with him, mingled together. At sight of him they set up such an imprecation on his head as if all the clustering cliffs had come crashing down in heaps. Here he was halloed when the men met with him, and loudly greeted with chiding cries; there he was threatened and often called thief, and ever the ticklers at his tail so that he might not tarry. Oft times he was chased when he made for the open, and oft times he swung in again, so wily was Reynard. And indeed after this fashion he led them a fine dance about the hills, the lord and his following, right till mid-morning, while the gracious knight sleeps soundly at home that cold morn within his comely curtains. But the lady, for love, did not let herself sleep or fail in the purpose so close to her heart. But she rose up promptly and made her way thither in a gay mantle reaching to the ground and handsomely furred with well trimmed skins. There were no goodly colours on her head, but well-wrought stones were set about her hair-net in clusters of twenty. Her lovely face and throat were laid all naked, her breast bare in front, her back bare too. She comes inside the chamber door and closes it after her, throws up a window and calls to the knight, and soon rallied him thus gaily with her winning words.

> 'Ah, sir, how mayst lie sleeping?
> The morning is so clear.'
> Deep he lay in slumber's maze,
> And yet her words can hear.

In the heavy oppression of dreams that noble knight lay muttering, as a man who was troubled with many grievous thoughts, how destiny must that day deal him his lot at the Green Chapel, when he meets his man and must needs stand his blow without more debate. But when that lovely lady came he recovered his senses, comes sharply out of his fantasies and makes speedy answer. The lady came lovingly and laughing sweetly, bent over his fair face and kissed him daintily. He gives her fair and fitting welcome. He saw her so glorious and gaily attired, so faultless of her parts and so finely coloured, that strong-welling joy warmed his heart. With mild gentle smiling they fell into gay speech, so that all was joy, happiness, and bliss which passed between them.

> The words they spoke were goodly,
> Much joy was there aright;
> Great peril had encompassed them
> Save Mary watch over her knight!

For that noble princess pressed him so close, urged him so near the limit, that he must needs accept her love or churlishly refuse it. He was troubled for his courtesy, lest he prove caitiff, and yet more for his ill-plight should he yield to sin and be traitor to that lord who ruled the castle. 'God forfend,' said the knight, 'that shall not befall.' With playful affection he set aside all the fond speeches that came from her lips. Said the lady to the knight: 'You deserve blame if you love not the creature you lie beside, wounded at heart before all women in the world, unless you have a mistress, a lady-love, who pleases you better, and have plighted troth to that lady, and knit so tight that it has no mind to release you. And I now believe that; and I pray you tell me that now truly, and for all the loves there are do not conceal the truth in guile.'

> The knight said, 'By Saint John,'
> Gently she saw him smile,
> 'In faith I enjoy none such,
> Nor will enjoy the while.'

'That is a word,' said the lady, 'which is worst of all. But I am answered indeed – and I think it pity. Kiss me now sweetly, and I shall go away. I can but mourn all my life, as one that greatly loves.' Sighing, she bent down and kissed him fairly, and thereafter draws apart from him, and says where she stands: 'Now, dear sir, do me this kindness at our parting: give me some gift of thine, thy glove as it might be, that I may remember thee, knight, to lessen my sorrow.' 'Now indeed', said the knight, 'for thy sake I wish I had here the most precious thing I own; for surely you have so often deserved more reward than I can rightly bestow. But to give for love's sake, that would be little use. It is not worthy of you to have now a glove of Gawain's gift for a keepsake; and I am here on a mission in unknown parts, and have no servants with baggage of things of worth. I am sorry for that, lady, for your sake at this time. But each man must do as he is circumstanced; so take no offence, nor pine.'

> 'Nay, fair sir,' said the lady,
> Under linen sweet and fine,
> 'Though I had naught of yours,
> Yet should you have of mine.'

She offered him a costly ring of red gold workmanship, with a blazing stone standing out therefrom which shot forth rays dazzling as the bright sun. Know well, it was of immense worth. But the knight refused it and said quickly, 'In God's name, I will have no gifts, dear lady, for the present. I have none to offer you, nor will I take any.' She presses it on him strongly, but he puts aside her offer, and swears swiftly by his troth that he would not accept it. And she was grieved that he denied her, and said thereafter, 'If you refuse my ring because it seems too costly and you would not be so highly beholden to me, I will give you my girdle, which profits you less.' Quickly she took hold of a belt which clasped her sides, fastened over her gown under the bright mantle. It was fashioned of green silk and outlined in gold, adorned at the edges only and embroidered by fingers. And she offered it to the knight and gaily urged that though it was unworthy of him yet he should accept it. And he said no, that he would in no wise touch either gold or treasure till God had sent him grace to make an end of the adventure for which he had set out thither. 'And therefore I pray you, be not displeased, and leave off what you are urging, for I can never bring myself to consent.

> 'I am much beholden to you
> Because of your fair treatment;
> And ever more in great and small
> Will be your faithful servant.'

'Now, do you reject this silk,' said the lady then, 'because it is simple in itself? And so indeed it seems. Lo, so it is little, and the less worthy of you. But whoever knew the virtues which are entwined therein, maybe he would esteem it of more price. For whoever is girt with this green lace, so long as he had it deftly tied about him there is no man under heaven might hew him down; for he might not be slain for any device upon earth.' Then the knight pondered, and it came into his heart how this were a jewel for the peril appointed him when he arrived at the Chapel to collect his ill winnings. Should he have escaped unslain, the stratagem were a noble one. Then he fell in with her importunity and suffered her to speak. And she pressed the belt on him, offering it continuously, and he consented, and she gave it him with right good will, and besought him for her sake never to make it known, but faithfully to conceal it from her lord. The knight indeed agrees that on no account should any ever know of it save they two.

> He thanked her oft and warmly,
> With heart and mind sincere;
> By then, not once but three times
> She has kissed the knight so dear.

Then she takes her leave and leaves him there, for she might not get more sport of that man. When she was gone, Sir Gawain at once makes ready, rises and garbs himself in noble array, lays up the love-lace the lady had given him, and hid it loyally where he might find it again. Thereafter he quickly made his way to the chapel, privately approached a priest and begged him there that he would raise his life and instruct him the better how his soul should be saved when he must go on his way hence. He confessed himself clean and laid bare his sins both the more and the less; and he begs for mercy and cries out on the priest for absolution. And he safely absolved him and left him as clean as if doomsday should be set for the morrow. And thereafter till the dark night, with courtly dances and joy of all kinds, he makes him as merry among those noble ladies as, save that day, he had never done yet.

> He charmed them each and all,
> Till man and woman say,
> 'He has not been so merry yet
> Since first he came our way.'

Now let him rest in that castle, where love betide him! The lord is still leading his men in the field. He has slain this fox which he long pursued. As he leapt over a thorn hedge to catch sight of the rascal, even as he heard the hounds which were hurrying on fast, Reynard came making his way through a rough thicket, and all the pack in a rush at his heels. The man was aware of the beast and waits warily, and plucks out his bright sword and flings it at the creature; and he flinched for the sharp weapon and would have drawn back. Before he might, a hound catches up with him, and right in front of the horse's feet they all fell on him and worried this wily one with a fierce uproar. Quickly the lord dismounts and at once grips hold of him, snatches him swiftly out of the dogs' mouths, holds him high over his head and halloes loudly, and many fierce hounds bay at him there. Huntsmen hastened thither with many a horn, blowing ever the recall till they might see their lord. When once this noble company was assembled, all who bore bugle there blew all together, and the rest halloed who had no horns. It was the merriest cry men ever heard, the noble clamour which was raised there for Reynard's soul.

> Their dogs they now reward there,
> They rub them, head and side,
> And afterwards take Reynard
> And strip him of his hide.

And then, because it was near to nightfall, they made for home, blowing lustily on their great horns. The lord lights down at last at his dear home, finds fire on the hall floor and the knight beside it, Sir Gawain the good, who was merry withal; he took much joy for friendship's sake among the ladies. He wore a robe of blue bleant which reached to the ground, his surcoat which was softly furred became him well, and a hood of the same stuff hung on his shoulder; both were adorned everywhere with blaunner. He meets the good lord in the middle of the floor, and merrily he greets him and said fairly: 'First I shall now fulfil our bargain which we discussed to our advantage when no drink was spared!' Then he embraces the knight and kisses him thrice with such relish and as steadfastly as he could lay on. 'By Christ,' declared the other knight, 'you get much happiness in winning this merchandise, if you bought in a good market.' 'Why, no matter for the market,' said the other quickly, 'since I have openly made over the wares that I had.' 'Mary,' said the other, 'mine lags behind, for I have hunted all this day and won nothing but this foul foxskin – devil take the thing! And that is poor payment indeed for such precious things as you have pressed warmly on me here, three kisses so good.'

> 'Enough,' cried Sir Gawain,
> 'I thank you, by the rood.'
> And how the fox was slain
> He told him as they stood.

With mirth and minstrelsy, with food to their taste, they made as merry as any men might, with laughter of ladies and jesting speeches. Gawain and the good lord were both of them so cheerful – unless the company would go too far or have grown drunk. Both lord and household played many a prank, till the time was come that they must part. Men must needs to their beds at last. Then this worthy man took leave first, and humbly, of the lord, and thanks him fairly. 'For such a wondrous stay as I have had here, your hospitality at this high feast, the King on High reward you. I offer myself to be your servant, if that please you, for as you know I must needs go my way tomorrow morning, if as you promised you appoint me some man to show me the way to the Green Chapel, even as God will suffer me to accept on New Year's day the verdict of my fate.' 'In good faith,' said that worthy lord, 'all that ever I promised you I shall hold to gladly.' He assigns a servant there to set him in the way and lead him through the hills, so that he experienced no trouble in riding through the forest and faring as was easiest through the woodland.

> Sir Gawain thanked the lord
> Who such kindness could conceive
> Then of those noble ladies
> The knight has taken leave.

With sorrow and kissing he talks with them, and he begged them to accept his warm abundant thanks. And they quickly requited him with just such words. Sighing unhappily, they commended him to Christ. Thereafter he took honourable leave of the household. Every one he met, he gave him thanks for his service and solicitude and the many pains they had been busied with to minister to him. And every one was as grieved to part with him as if they had for ever dwelt in honour with that noble knight. Then he was conducted to his chamber with men and light, and joyously brought to bed to take his rest. Whether he slept soundly or not I dare not tell, for if he chose he had much on his mind for the morning.

> Let him lie there quiet,
> He has near what he sought;
> Be patient yet a little while,
> I shall tell you how they wrought.

4

NOW THE NEW YEAR DRAWS NEAR and the night passes; the day gains on the dark, as the Lord biddeth. But fierce storms spring thereout in the world; clouds cast the cold piercingly to the ground, with harm enough from the north to grieve the naked. The snow shook down full bitterly and nipped the wild creatures; the whistling wind came in gusts from the heights and drove each valley full of great drifts. The man lying in his bed listened closely; though he shuts his eyelids he sleeps but little. By every cock that crew he knew well his hour. Ere the day sprang he rose betimes, for there was light from a lamp which shone in his chamber. He called to his chamberlain who answered him briskly, and bade him bring his mail-shirt and his steed's saddle. The other bestirs him and fetches his gear, and Sir Gawain arrays himself bravely. First he clad him in his clothes to keep out the cold, and afterwards his other harness which had been faithfully tended, both his paunce and his steel plate burnished clean, the rings of his good mail-shirt rocked free of rust. And it was all as fresh as when new, and he was desirous then to thank them.

> He donned each piece of armour,
> So fairly polished at need;
> The gayest from here to Greece,
> The knight bade bring his steed.

But while he drew on him his handsome raiment, his cote-armure with its device of lovely workmanship, precious stones as a border to the velvet, worked and bound, its seams embroidered, and handsomely lined within with fair furs, he yet did not overlook the lace, the lady's gift. For his own sake Gawain did not forget that. When he had belted the sword on his smooth hips, he then arranged his love-token double about him; quickly and gladly the knight wrapped about his middle the girdle of green silk, which well became that gallant man over royal red cloth which was rich to view. But the knight did not wear this girdle for its costliness, for pride of its pendants though they were polished, and though glittering gold shone at the edges; but to save himself when he must needs suffer and abide death without swordplay or dagger to protect him.

> And now the knight in armour
> Is ready to depart;
> The many proud retainers,
> He thanks them from his heart.

Then Gringolet was ready, who was tall and huge, and had been tended to his liking and safely. That proud steed wished to gallop, he was in such fettle. The knight goes up to him and looks at his coat, spoke with measured words, and swears by his troth, 'Within this moat is a household which is mindful of honour. As for the lord who maintains them, joy may he have! The dear lady, all her life may love be her lot. If they of their charity cherish a guest and have honour in their keeping, may the Lord who rules heaven above repay them, and all of you too! And if I might stay alive any while, readily should I find you some reward, were I permitted.' Then he steps into the stirrup and mounts aloft. His squire showed him his shield, he took it on his shoulder, spurs Gringolet with his gilded heels, and he sprang forward on the stones; no longer would he stand and prance.

> His guide was then on horseback,
> Who bore his spear and lance.
> 'This castle I commend to Christ.'
> He bade it ever good chance.

The bridge was let down and the wide gates unbarred and borne open on both sides. The knight crossed himself quickly and passed over the planks. He praises the porter, who knelt before the prince and wished him godspeed and good-day that He should save Gawain, and he went on his way with his one companion who should direct him to make for that grievous place where he must abide the pitiless onslaught. They rode by hillsides where boughs are bare; they climbed past cliffs where the cold clings. The clouds were uplifted but ugly thereunder. Mist drizzled on the moor, melted on the mountains. Each hill had a hat, a great hackle of mist. Brooks boiled and broke about the hillsides, dashing brightly against the banks where they thrust their way down. Most puzzling was the way they must fare through the forest, till presently it was the hour when the sun rises.

> They were on a lofty hill,
> White snow around them lay;
> The guide who rode beside him
> Now bade his master stay.

'For I have now brought you hither, sir, and you are this moment not far from that noted place you have sought and asked after so particularly. But now that I know you, and you are a man I love well, truly I shall tell you that if you were to follow my counsel you would fare the better. The place you are hastening to is held most perilous. In that desolate spot dwells the worst man on earth; for he is grim and strong and loves to deal blows, and he is bigger than any man alive, and his body huger than the best four that are in Arthur's household, Hector, or any other. He brings it to pass at the Green Chapel that none so proud in arms rides by that place that he does not smite him dead with a blow of his hand. For he is a violent man and shows no mercy; for whether it be churl or chaplain who rides past the Chapel, or monk or masspriest or any man else, he thinks it as pleasant to slay him as stay alive himself. Therefore I tell thee, as sure as you sit in saddle, come there and you will be killed if the knight may have his way – yea, believe me, though you had twenty lives to spend.

> 'He has sojourned here so long now,
> His mischief has been immense;
> Against his heavy, grievous blows
> You cannot make defence.

'Therefore, good Sir Gawain, let the man be, and depart by some other road, in God's name. Ride through some other land, where Christ speed you, and I shall hasten back home, and I promise you further that I shall swear by God and all his good saints, so help me God and his holy relics and oaths enough, that I shall keep your secret loyally and never breathe word that to my knowledge you ever took to flight for any man.' 'I thank thee,' said Gawain, and he spoke with distaste. 'Good luck to thee, fellow, for wishing me well. And I well believe thou wouldst keep my secret loyally. But though thou kept it never so faithfully, if I passed by here, brought to flight for fear in the fashion thou tellest of, I were a coward knight and might not be excused. But I shall proceed to the Chapel despite what may befall, and speak with that same man the word I please, come of it weal or woe, even as fate is pleased to have it.

> 'Though he be a grim fellow
> To manage, with his stave,
> Our Lord can find a ready way
> His servants true to save.'

'Mary!' vowed the other man, 'now thou goest so far as to say thou wilt bring down on thyself thine own harm, and since it pleases thee lose thy life, I care not to hinder thee. Take here thy helm on thy head, thy spear in thy hand, and ride down this same path by yonder cliff-side till thou be brought to the bottom of the rugged valley. Then look some way off in the clearing to thy left hand, and thou shalt see in that hollow the Chapel itself, and the mighty man there who maintains it. Now fare well in God's name, noble Gawain! I would not go with thee for all the gold in the world, nor keep thee company one foot further through this forest.' With that the fellow turns his bridle into the wood, pricked his horse with his heels as hard as he could, gallops over the clearing, and leaves the knight there all alone.

> 'By God's Own Self,' vowed Gawain,
> 'I will neither groan nor weep;
> I submit me fully to His will;
> I trust He will me keep.'

Then he spurs Gringolet and picks up the path, thrust in by a cliff at a thicket's side, rides across the rough slope right to the valley. And then he looked about him, and wild it seemed to him; and he saw no sign of a dwelling anywhere there, but high steep banks on both sides, and rough rugged crags with gnarled stones. The very clouds appeared to him grazed by the rocks. He then tarried and reined in his horse for a while, and looked often this way and that to find the Chapel. He saw none such on any side, and wondrous he thought it – save some way off in the clearing a mound as it were, a smooth round barrow on a bank beside the water's edge, by the fall of a stream that ran there. The brook bubbled therein as though it had boiled. The knight urges on his horse and came to the mound, alights fairly down, and ties the rein to a tree and secured it with a rough branch. Then he makes his way to the barrow and walks round it, debating with himself what it might be. It had a hole at the end and on either side, and was everywhere overgrown with clumps of grass, and was all hollow within, nothing but an old cave or crevice of an old crag, he could not tell which.

> 'Alas, Lord,' said the gentle knight,
> 'Is this the Green Chapel?
> Here indeed about midnight
> Might the devil his matins tell!

'Now in faith,' vowed Gawain, 'it is dreary here! This oratory is ugly, overgrown with vegetation. It well suits the man garbed in green to perform his devotions here in devilish wise. Now I feel in my five senses it is the Fiend who has imposed on me this tryst, to destroy me here. This is a chapel of mischance, ill luck take it! It is the cursedest church that ever I entered.' With towering helm on his head, his lance in his hand, he roams up to the roof of those unkempt quarters. Then he heard from that high hill, in a hard rock beyond the brook, a wondrous fierce noise. What! it clattered in the cliff as though it should split, as though one were grinding a scythe on a grindstone. What! it whirred and it whetted like water in a mill. What! it rushed and it rang, grievous to hear. Then, 'By God,' said Gawain, 'that gear, so I fancy, sir, is made ready in honour of meeting me in my turn.

> 'God's will be done! Alas,
> This helps me not at all.
> But though I lose my life,
> No noise shall me appal.'

Then the knight called aloud: 'Who is master here, to hold tryst with me? For now the good Gawain is walking right here. If any one desire aught, let him come hither fast to do what he has to, either now or never.' 'Wait,' said one on the hillside up over his head, 'and thou shalt speedily have all I once promised thee.' Yet he went briskly on for a while with that rushing noise, and turned back to his whetting ere he would descend. And afterwards he makes his way past a crag and comes out of a hole, whirling out of a corner with a fell weapon, a new-made danish axe with which to return the blow, with a mighty cutting-edge curving along the handle, sharpened on a grindstone, four foot wide (it was no less by that lace which gleamed so bright); and the man in green arrayed as at first, both face and legs, hair and beard, save that he strides fairly over the ground on foot, set the handle to the rock and stalked beside it. When he reached the water, where he had no wish to wade, he hopped across on his axe and strides stoutly over the snow, fiercely fell on a field that stretched wide about.

> Sir Gawain went to meet the knight,
> He would neither greet nor sue;
> The other said, 'Why now, sweet sir,
> To your tryst I find you true.

'Gawain,' said the Green Knight, 'God keep thee! In faith thou art welcome, sir, to my place, and thou hast timed thy journey as a true man should. Thou knowest the covenants set between us; this time twelvemonth thou didst take what fell thy way, and this New Year I should speedily requite thee. And in this valley we are most assuredly on our own. No men are here to separate us, reel as we like. Take thy helm from thy head, and have here thy pay. Show no more resistance than I offered then, when thou didst whip off my head at a stroke.' 'Nay,' declared Gawain, 'by God who gave me spirit, I shall bear thee no ill will for the harm that befalls. But set yourself to one blow, and I shall stand still and show thee no resistance for doing as thou please, anywhere.'

> He bowed his neck, and bending
> He showed the flesh all bare;
> No sign was seen of his dismay,
> Nor would he flinch for fear.

Then the man in green quickly made ready and lifts up his grim tool to smite Gawain. With all the strength in his body he swings it aloft, feinted as mightily as though he would destroy him. Had it crashed down as hard as he aimed, then he who was ever valiant knight had died of his blow. But Gawain looked sideways on that gisarme as it came gliding down to earth to make an end of him, and shrank a little with his shoulders for the sharp iron. With a jerk the other checks the bright blade, and he then reproaches the prince with many high words. 'Thou art not Gawain,' said the knight, 'who is esteemed so good, who never quailed for an army by hill or vale – and now thou art flinching for fear ere thou feel hurt. Such cowardice I might never hear of that knight. I neither flinched nor fled, sir, when thou tookst aim at me, nor raised any quibble in king Arthur's house. My head flew to my foot, and still I never fled. And thou, ere any harm taken, growest fearful of heart. For that reason then I must needs be called the better man.'

> Said Gawain, 'I flinched once,
> And so will I no more;
> But if my head fall on the stones,
> I cannot it restore.

'But make ready, sir, by thy faith, and come to the point with me. Deal me my doom, and do it out of hand, for I shall stand a stroke of thine and start no more till thine axe has struck me. Take here my plighted word.' 'Have at thee then!' said the other, and heaves it on high,. and showed as angry as if he were mad. He feints at him strongly but does not touch the man; he suddenly checked his hand ere it might do hurt. Gawain duly awaits it and flinched in no member, but stood still as a stone or a stock which is entwined in rocky ground with a hundred roots. Then merrily he spoke thereafter, the man in green: 'So! Now thou hast thy heart whole, I must needs lay on. Let the fine knighthood which Arthur gave thee save thee now and keep thy windpipe at this stroke, if it may avail.' 'Why,' said Gawain wrathfully and in anger then, 'lay on, thou heartless man! Thou threatenest too long. I fancy thy heart grows fearful of thine own self.' 'In truth,' declared the other, 'thou speakest so angrily, I will no longer now leave thine errand in arrears.'

> He then takes stance to strike him,
> And puckers mouth and brow;
> No wonder this mispleased him
> Who saw no rescue now.

He lifts his weapon swiftly and let it down bravely, with the edge of the blade on the bare neck. Though he struck fiercely, it did him no more injury than to nick him on that one side, which severed the skin. The sharp axe shrank into the flesh through the shining fat, so that the bright blood shot over his shoulders to the ground. And when the knight saw the blood gleam on the snow, he sprang away with feet out-kicked more than a spear's length, quickly caught up his helm and set it on his head, and with his shoulders swung under his fair shield, plucks out his bright sword and fiercely he speaks. Never since he was born of his mother was he man so blithe in this world. 'Cease, sir, your striking. Offer me no more. I have taken a stroke in this place without fight, and if you proffer me any more I shall make swift requital and return it promptly and cruelly, be sure of that!

> 'But one stroke is my portion,
> Such was our bargain of yore,
> Confirmed in Arthur's royal hall
> – And therefore, sir, no more!'

The knight drew off from him and rested on his axe; he set the haft to ground and leaned on his weapon, and watched how the man moved on that level ground, how the brave knight stands boldly there, unafraid in arms, and dauntless. It pleased him in his heart. Then he speaks merrily with a great voice, and in ringing tones he said to the knight, 'Brave sir, be not so fierce in this place. No one has used thee ill here, nor acted save according to the agreement shaped at Arthur's court. I promised thee a stroke, and thou hast had it. Consider thyself well paid. I release thee from the residue of all dues else. Had I been keen, maybe I could have dealt a buffet more harshly, to cause thee anger. First I threatened thee jovially, with a feint only, and did not even wound thee with a cut — which I offered thee of right for the bargain we struck the first night; and thou keptst with me in trust and truth our compact and gave me all the winnings, as a good man should. The other feint, sir, I offered thee for the morrow: thou didst kiss my fair wife and render me the kisses. For those two I offered thee here but two simple feints, with no harm done.

> 'Let true man true restore,
> Then he need fear no woe;
> The third time thou didst fare amiss,
> And therefore take that blow!

'For it is my raiment thou wearest, that same woven girdle. My own wife gave it thee, and well I know it. Aye, I know all about thy kisses, and thy behaviour too, and the wooing of my wife. I myself wrought it. I sent her to try thee – truly, as I think, the most faultless man that ever trod. As a pearl is of more price compared with a white pea, so is Gawain, in good faith, compared with other gay knights. But here you fell away a little, sir, and came short in loyalty. But that was for no choice embroidery, nor the wooing either, but because you loved your life – I blame you the less!' The other bold man stood a long while in silent thought, so grieved with vexation that he groaned within him. All the blood flowed together from his breast to his face, so that he shrank for shame at what the lord told of. The very first word the man spoke: 'Cursed be cowardice and greed too! In you is baseness, and vice which destroys virtue.' Then he snatched at the knot and unties the twist, angrily flung the belt to the lord himself. 'Lo, the false thing there, ill betide it! Through anxiety as to thy blow cowardice taught me to make terms with greed, and to forsake my true nature, which is liberality and loyalty such as befit knights. Now I am faulty and false, and have ever been afraid of treachery and faithlessness. Sorrow and care befall both!

> 'I confess it here between us,
> With error did I fare
> But let me know your will,
> I shall next time take more care.'

Then the other man laughed and said in friendly wise: 'The hurt that I had, I hold it wholly amended. Thou art confessed so clean, and thy faults acknowledged, and thou hast the clear penance of my weapon's point. I hold thee cleansed of that offence, and purified as clear as though thou hadst never sinned since the day thou wast born. And I give thee, sir, the girdle hemmed with gold, for it is green as my gown. Sir Gawain, you may think on this same contention where thou shalt press forth among renowned princes, and this is a sure token for chivalrous knights of the adventure of the Green Chapel. And this New Year you shall return again to my dwelling, and we will revel away the rest of this noble festival.'

> The lord pressed Gawain hard,
> Said, 'With my wife, I know,
> We can bring you yet to terms,
> Who was one time your foe.'

'Nay, truly,' declared the knight, and he took hold of his helm and removes it courteously, and thanks his host. 'I have made a sorry stay. Fortune betide you, and may He grant it you fully who ordains all honours. And commend me to that gracious one, your lovely wife – both the one and the other, my honoured ladies, who with their stratagem have thus neatly beguiled their knight. But it is no marvel though a fool run mad and be brought to grief through women's wiles. For so was Adam beguiled with one upon earth, and Solomon with only too many. And Samson again, Dalila dealt him his weird; and David thereafter, who suffered much woe, was deluded by Bathsheba. Since these were brought to grief with their wiles, it were great joy to love them well but believe them not, the man who could. For these, whom all good fortune followed, were in days gone by pre-eminently the noblest of all these others who mused under heaven.

> 'And they were all ensnared
> By women whom they used.
> Though in my turn beguiled,
> I think I may be excused.

'But your girdle,' said Gawain, 'God repay you! That I will have with good will, not for the lovely gold, nor the ceinture nor the silk, nor the wide pendants, neither for joy nor honour, nor for the handsome embroidery; but when I ride in glory I shall see it often as the sign of my transgression, and remorsefully remember the fault and the frailty of the crabbed flesh, how tender it is to take infection of vileness. And so, when pride shall incite me for prowess in arms, the sight of this love-lace shall humble my heart. But one thing I would ask of you, if it displease you not. Since you are lord of yonder country where I have dwelt with you in honour – may He repay you who upholds the heavens and sits on high! – how call you your right name, and then no more?' 'That I shall tell you truly,' declared the other then. 'Bertilak de Hautdesert am I called in this country, through the might of Morgan la Faye, who lives in my house, and her cunning in magic, by crafts well learned. She has acquired many of Merlin's arts, for upon a time she has had love-dealings full dear with that susceptible sage, as all your knights at home know.

> 'Morgan the goddess,
> This therefore is her name;
> There is no one of such lofty pride
> But she can make him tame.

'She sent me in this wise to your fair hall to make trial of its pride, whether it were true, the great renown that runs of the Round Table. She cast on me this enchantment to reave you of your wits, in order to have grieved Guenevere and made her die of dismay at that selfsame creature that spoke so ghastly with his head in his hand before the high table. That is she who is at home, the aged lady. She is none other than thine aunt, Arthur's half-sister, daughter of the duchess of Tintagel on whom the valiant Uther afterwards begot Arthur, who is now so noble. And so I entreat thee, knight, come to thine aunt, make merry at my home; my household loves thee, and I wish thee well, sir, by my faith, as any man alive, for thy honest dealing.' But he gave him nay for an answer, would by no means consent. They embrace and kiss and commend each other to the Prince of Paradise, and part there on the cold ground.

> Sir Gawain on his gallant steed
> To the king's court rides boldly;
> And that same knight in vivid green
> Whithersoever would he.

Wild ways in the world rides Gawain now on Gringolet, a man dowered with the gift of his life. Oft times he lodged within doors, oft times without, and more than once he escaped many a peril in the vale which I do not propose to recount just now in story. The wound he had taken in his neck was healed, and he wore about it the gleaming belt, cross-wise as a baldric bound to his side, and the lace fastened under his left arm with a knot, in token that he was taken in blemish of a fault. And thus he comes to court, a knight all whole. There was joy roused in that dwelling when its lord knew that the good Gawain was come; great gain it seemed to him. The king kisses the knight, and the queen likewise; and thereafter there was many a true knight that sought to embrace him and asked him how he had fared. And a wondrous tale he tells, and confesses all the hardships that he had, the adventure of the Chapel, the knight's behaviour, the love of the lady, and at last of the lace. He laid bare for them the nick in his neck which he obtained at the lord's hand in rebuke for his disloyalty.

> He grieved when he must tell it,
> He groaned for the disgrace;
> When he must reveal his shame,
> The blood rushed to his face.

'Lo, sire,' said the knight, and he took the lace in hand, 'this is the emblazonry of this fault I bear on my neck. This is the offence and the loss I have taken of the cowardice and greed I caught there. This is the token of the faithlessness I am taken in, and I must needs wear it so long as I live. For no one can hide his hurt, lest misfortune follow, for where once it is attached it will never be undone.' The king comforts the knight, and all the court too laugh loudly thereat, and in their courtesy agree that lords and ladies belonging to the Round Table should have, each one of the brotherhood, a baldric, a band of bright green cross-wise about him, and wear it to match, for that knight's sake. For it was accorded the renown of the Round Table, and he that had it honoured ever after, even as it is set down in the best book of romance. And thus in Arthur's day this adventure befell: the Brutus books bear witness to it. Since that bold man Brutus first came hither after the siege and the assault were ended at Troy, trust to it,

> Many adventures of this sort
> Have fallen out ere this.
> Now He that wore the crown of thorns
> Bring us to His bliss!

Hony Soyt qui Mal Pence

Glossary

Avanters: part of the numbles of the deer.
Aventail: the movable mouthpiece of a helmet *or* chain-mail dependent from the chin to the upper breast.
Blaunner (or Blaunmer): a white (?) fur.
Bleant: a rich fabric.
Caroles: dances combined with song.
Cote-armure: a coat or vest, showing a knight's coat-of-arms, worn over the armour.
Erber: the first stomach of ruminants.
Gisarme: a spiked battle-axe.
Kenet: a harrier, a small hunting dog.
Molaynes: bridle-studs *or* bit-studs.
Numbles: part of the offal of the deer.
Paunce: armour covering the abdomen.
Paytrure: the breast-harness of a horse.
Pysan: armour for the upper breast and neck.
Polaynes: knee-pieces.
Sabatouns: steel shoes.
Sendal: a fine silk.
Singler: a full grown boar which has left the herd.

WORDSWORTH CLASSICS
OF WORLD LITERATURE

AESCHYLUS
The Oresteia

APULEIUS
The Golden Ass

ARISTOTLE
The Nicomachean Ethics

MARCUS AURELIUS
Meditations

FRANCIS BACON
Essays

JAMES BOSWELL
The Life of Samuel Johnson
(ABRIDGED)

JOHN BUNYAN
The Pilgrim's Progress

CATULLUS
Poems

CARL VON CLAUSEWITZ
On War
(ABRIDGED)

CONFUCIUS
The Analects

DANTE ALIGHIERI
The Inferno

CHARLES DARWIN
The Origin of Species
The Voyage of the Beagle

RENÉ DESCARTES
Key Philosophical Writings

DESIDERIUS ERASMUS
Praise of Folly

SIGMUND FREUD
The Interpretation of Dreams

EDWARD GIBBON
*The Decline and Fall of the
Roman Empire*
(ABRIDGED)

KAHLIL GIBRAN
The Prophet

HERODOTUS
Histories

THOMAS HOBBES
Leviathan

HORACE
The Odes

KENKO
Essays in Idleness

T. E. LAWRENCE
Seven Pillars of Wisdom

JOHN LOCKE
*Essay Concerning Human
Understanding*
(ABRIDGED)

NICCOLO MACHIAVELLI
The Prince

SIR THOMAS MALORY
Le Morte Darthur

JOHN STUART MILL
*On Liberty & The Subjection
of Women*